The Social Theory of Practices

The Social Theory of Practices
Tradition, Tacit Knowledge and Presuppositions

Stephen Turner

Polity Press

Copyright © Stephen Turner 1994.

The right of Stephen Turner to be identified as author of this work has been asserted in accordance with the Copyright, Designs and Patents Act 1988.

First published in 1994 by Polity Press
in association with Blackwell Publishers

Editorial office:
Polity Press
65 Bridge Street
Cambridge CB2 1UR, UK

Marketing and production:
Blackwell Publishers
108 Cowley Road
Oxford OX4 1JF, UK

All rights reserved. Except for the quotation of short passages for the purposes of criticism and review, no part of this publication may be reproduced, stored in a retrieval system, or transmitted, in any form or by any means, electronic, mechanical, photocopying, recording or otherwise, without the prior permission of the publisher.

Except in the United States of America, this book is sold subject to the condition that it shall not, by way of trade or otherwise, be lent, re-sold, hired out, or otherwise circulated without the publisher's prior consent in any form of binding or cover other than that in which it is published and without a similar condition including this condition being imposed on the subsequent purchaser.

ISBN 0–7456 0504–4
ISBN 0–7456 1372–1 (pbk)

British Library Cataloguing-in-Publication Data
A CIP catalogue record for this book is available from the British Library.

Typeset in 10 on 12pt Times
by Best-set Typesetters Ltd., Hong Kong

This book is printed on acid-free paper.

To Kim

Contents

Acknowledgements ix

1 Practices and their Conceptual Kin 1
2 Practices as Causes 14
3 Practices as Presuppositions 28
4 Transmission 44
5 Change and History 78
6 The Opacity of Practice 101

Notes 124
Index 137

Acknowledgements

Philosophy, as I think of it, is a form of atonement for past enthusiasms. This book is the product of a long struggle with myself over the ideas of tradition and practice, and particularly with the inadequacies of my own *Sociological Explanation as Translation* (Cambridge University Press, 1980). The work was originally motivated by my attraction to these ideas and my respect for, and enjoyment of, the works of Michael Oakeshott, Michael Polanyi, H.-G. Gadamer and Alasdair MacIntyre. My interest in the subject was mediated personally by the tutelage of J.P. Mayer, Edward Shils and Richard Rorty. Originally, I wished to make a contribution to the tradition of conceptualizations of 'tradition'. Instead, I have argued for its dissolution, at least in its standard forms. The petty forms of these ideas, ideas such as 'social constructionism', fall in the range of the argument I have made here as well. So does much else.

The book has benefited greatly from the generosity of others. Paul Roth, Mike Lynch, Bert Rolf, Ray Scupin, Tom Ross, Steve Fuller and Andy Pickering made extensive and useful comments, and raised many questions. I have, I am afraid, answered only a few of them. I was also helped by two institutions. I cadged time from a National Endowment for the Humanities Fellowship. But most crucial was the time I spent at the Swedish Collegium for Advanced Studies in the Social Sciences. In

x *Acknowledgements*

addition to the opportunity to concentrate on this project, I had the benefit of advice from two other SCASSS fellows, Göran Ahrne and Jeff Alexander. Corrections for the final draft were entered by Norma Walker.

1
Practices and their Conceptual Kin

> But I did not get my picture of the world by satisfying myself of its correctness; nor do I have it because I am satisfied of its correctness. No: it is the inherited background against which I distinguish between true and false.[1]

> Heidegger argues that ... even when people act deliberately, and so have beliefs, plans, follow rules, etc., their minds cannot be directed toward something except on a background of shared social practices.[2]

Practices, it would appear, are the vanishing point of twentieth-century philosophy. The major philosophical achievements of the century are now widely interpreted as assertions about practices, even though they were not originally couched in this language. The first epigraph, from Wittgenstein, is explained in a recent book as follows: 'Wittgenstein argues that one's convictions depend upon, and make sense only within a largely tacit picture of the world that one inherits unavoidably as a member of a given community.'[3] The second epigraph is from the major English-language interpreter of Heidegger, Hubert Dreyfus, who has chosen in his major work to account for Heidegger's central idea of *Dasein* in terms of the concept of *habitus* popularized by the sociologist Pierre Bourdieu.[4] Wittgenstein himself borrowed the notion of *Lebensformen* from a philosopher and sociologist, Eduard Spranger.

The vanishing point, then, is in a domain traditionally belonging to social theory. But the use of the term 'practices' is far more widespread. The appeal to 'the diversity of human practices', as Edward Said puts it, is standard in the humanities. In literary criticism, feminist scholarship, rhetorical analysis and studies of the discourse of science, texts are routinely analysed in terms of the rhetorical practices and practices of representation they employ. The analyses are taken to explain such things as the construction of texts, their effects on readers and the reproduction of distinctions, such as gendering distinctions. The term appears in 'hard' contexts too, for example in artificial intelligence,

2 Practices and their Conceptual Kin

where it is used to describe field-specific cognitive competencies to be modelled, such as the body of legal practices that enables a lawyer to read a contract. Historians, anthropologists and other social scientists routinely use the notion in interpreting other cultures and times. 'Practice theory' is a major current in anthropological theory, where the term is used in opposition to the older emphases on belief, ritual and language.[5]

But the concept is deeply elusive. What are 'practices'? What is being referred to, for example, by Wittgenstein's phrase 'the inherited background against which I distinguish between true and false'? What are 'tacit pictures of the world'? These are not everyday objects. And they are given additional, mysterious properties – they are said to be 'shared', or 'social'. How seriously should we take this language? Are there really objectifiable things that we should think of as being shared or inherited? Or are these merely figures of speech? And if so, why should we be willing to accept them as part of the explanation of anything as central as truth or intentionality? What do they stand for that enables them to play this kind of central role in our thought?

This book was originally conceived as an answer to these questions. I realized from the outset that my quarry was necessarily broader than the concept of practices. I saw that there was a large family of terms that were used more or less interchangeably with 'practices'. Among them were some of the most widely used terms in philosophy and the humanities, such as tradition, tacit knowledge, *Weltanschauung*, paradigm, ideology, framework and presupposition. The insight that the people of earlier epochs had different visions of the world is at the core of historical relativism, and at the core of postmodernism, which rejects the claims to ultimate validity of any given vision of the world or practice of representing the world. That historicism was the source of some of these usages was common knowledge. But beyond this the history was murky, and the connections between various usages was unclear.

My first instinct was to think that some clarity could be produced by systematically identifying the variant forms of these ideas. In the literature of philosophy, in addition to Wittgenstein's allusion to 'the inherited background' and Kuhn's concept of paradigm, one might cite Oakeshott's comments on traditions and what they are not, Polanyi's concept of 'tacit knowledge', Ryle's distinction between 'knowing how' and 'knowing that', MacIntyre's and Gadamer's uses of the concept of tradition, 'practices' in Richard Rorty, Quine's notion of a person's 'theory of the world' (part of which is presumably tacit), David Lewis' notion of conventions without conveners, Elster's culture-specific norms that 'can exist on an unconscious or barely conscious level', and Unger's 'reasonless routines'.[6]

These concepts have affinities to one another, to be sure. Some of the concepts overlap one another or indeed are indistinguishable. But there seems to be a difference between two groups of concepts – those that are based on the model of hidden premisses of deductive theories, 'shared presuppositions', and those that refer to embodied knowledge, such as skills, ingrained cultural or moral dispositions, or linguistic competencies. But many of the concepts in the family fall into neither group. Indeed, the appeal of many of these concepts rests on the fact that they neglect this distinction or trespass against it. Kuhn's notion of paradigm, like Polanyi's notion of tacit knowledge, trades on the interdependence of skill and presupposition that is part of the scientist's way. The phrase 'inscribed on the body', common among French writers on these subjects, captures the duality of these concepts – discursive and corporal at once.

The list I gave above includes concepts with some current significance in philosophy. But as I have suggested, the many kindred concepts are originally from social thought, and the traffic in concepts has gone both ways. Some of these concepts were warmly embraced by 'social scientists' and employed in place of previously fashionable concepts. 'Paradigm', for example, was often used in the social sciences as a polite, legitimizing term in place of 'ideology'. Other terms were simply appropriated from or shared with social science or, in the case of tradition, with other bodies of thought, such as theology, law and politics, which had established their usages long before there were 'social sciences'. In this larger 'family' there are forms of the concepts that fit with neither the 'presuppositions' nor the 'embodiment' model. 'Tradition' and 'custom', for example, may describe a long historical series of imitative public enactments, a set of recognized legal rights, or the externals of a way of life, in which there is no element that is either presupposed or embodied.

'Practices' in the history of ideas

Nineteenth-century philosophy and social theory employed most of these ideas, in slightly different forms. But in the nineteenth century the concepts did not have the same range of uses. By the early part of the twentieth century, 'culture' and 'norms' were used to account for intractable differences of moral opinion. Those whose views one previously found to be admirable or despicable could be seen to be the product of divergent social norms or a different culture. In this form the terms served to undermine, or reflected the undermining of, moral and political certitudes. By showing the historically situated character of the 'norms' in question, the language of norms raised the question of whether our own deepest convictions were after all merely social conventions. Showing the connection between normative beliefs and concealed self-interests led to the question of whether conventional morality was a kind of plot whose beneficiaries, such as the bourgeoisie, could be identified. These ideas were no less threatening than postmodernism appears today.

The terminology, and the threat, was largely confined to morals and political belief. But there were some interesting exceptions to the limitation of these concepts to morality. Sociologists in the early part of the century sometimes spoke of the *mores* of a scientific society, which indicated that they considered science itself to be a normatively governed product of social evolution. This idea plays a role in Spencer, who also contributed the idea that moral intuitions are themselves the product of social evolution. The idea that scientific modes of thinking are in some sense obligatory in modern society in domains other than science can be discerned in pragmatism, and is even to be found in such thinkers as Parsons. The evolutionism of these thinkers protected them from reflexive contradiction: the *mores* of a scientific society were their *mores*, and they were the most evolutionarily advanced *mores* available.

The logical positivists had no objections to even the most extreme forms of sociological reductionism, if it was applied to morals. For them, the fact – value distinction was a fire-wall that prevented sociological reductionism from reaching science. Cultural relativists cheerfully conceded the relativity of their own society's moral ideas and customs. But at the same time, and for much the same reasons, they did not consider anthropology or behavioural science itself to be merely another culture. The main critics of this comfortable assumption were Marxist critical theorists practising the 'sociology of knowledge' who had a view of historical development in which 'bourgeois' social science was destined for the dustbin of history along with bourgeois society. But the critical theorists comforted themselves with the thought that their own views were historically progressive and therefore would be validated by the coming revolution – however delayed it might be.

This reasoning too had deep nineteenth-century roots. The idea of historically variable presuppositions was central to neo-Kantianism, as it was to the historical writings of Burckhardt, to Hegel's quest for the Spirit animating the development of Roman law, and to Hegel's historical critics, such as the philosopher of law Rudolph von Ihering, who himself was deeply influenced by neo-Kantianism. But the neo-Kantians themselves for the most part did not grasp the relativizing implications of the idea. They were still Kantian enough to suppose, typically, that there were matters of form that were historically invariant and thus the proper subject of, for example, ethics.

The present use of the concept of practices and its variants reflects the disappearance of the fire-wall between fact and value and the demise of evolutionism of the Marxian variety. But the ground was well prepared. The concept of tradition, historical world-view and custom had a central role as well in 'classical social theory' – the writings of Weber, Durkheim and their contemporaries, notably Ferdinand Tönnies.[7] The common source for these thinkers was Ihering, who gave an evolutionary account of the evolution of the tacit *Sitten* (morally binding customs) that underlie social life and without which legal order would be impossible. Ihering attempted to systematically classify and distinguish between morality, custom and other evolving social usages, but without much success. Weber was moved to redefine the concept of *Sitte* for the purposes of his sociology to avoid any suggestion that *Sitten* were shared mental objects of the sort Ihering had in mind. Durkheim, in contrast, embraced the idea that there were shared mental objects and raised them to the level of a novel realm of 'social' fact.[8]

The political theorists and historians of the nineteenth century had more to say about concepts in the 'practices' family than either the social theorists or philosophers. This was the era of constitutionalism and a time when the failure of transplanted democratic forms to thrive was part of the common experience of Continental intellectuals. Taine's reflections on the subject used the image of the rooting of a tree, and concluded that the tree of democracy would not root in soil that was not prepared by appropriate traditions. The idea was central to the celebration of the British constitution and the tracing of Anglo-Saxon origins of political and legal institutions, such as the common law. The aficionados of Anglo-Saxon origins wrote as though a millennia of experience with the 'moot' was a precondition for a free political order. Some of this thinking came close to a more disturbing mysticism of race and blood, a mysticism to which the Germans later succumbed. But the constitutionalists had a point – underlined by the two world wars of the twentieth century as well as the repeated failure of attempts to build liberal constitutional regimes in nineteenth-century Europe –

Democratic forms placed on non-democratic political cultures produced dangerous results.

As the classical social theorists saw, claims about political culture could not easily be formulated in a way consistent with our knowledge of the causal workings of the world. Sumner, who used the term *mores* to describe these deep cultural forces, had trouble explaining how they came about and why they varied from society to society. The problems about causality are overwhelming: if a culture is a causal object, how does it work, and what kind of object is it? So the legacy of the nineteenth century is a problem about practices, a problem about their status as objects, their causal properties and their 'collective' character – a problem which is unresolved and casts a shadow over the present uses of the term. The classical social theorists did not solve these problems. Freudianism and behaviourism helped, in different ways, in the evasion of these problems. The questions of why moral ideas seem to have a kind of force or compulsion over us and seem 'external' were resolved, to the extent that they were resolved, by the Freudian imagery of a super-ego constituted by introjected parental commands. The behaviourists made it simpler – they rejected theorizing about mental objects. For them, socialization was a matter of measurable external facts.

Earlier uses of the concepts in this family show why this kind of solution is overly facile. The relation between 'custom' and 'nature', which has puzzled thinkers since antiquity, is one obstacle to any such simple reduction. Hobbes said that 'manners maketh man'. Pascal varied an aphorism of Cicero to the effect that 'custom is second nature' with the remark that perhaps 'nature itself is but a first custom'. The language is instructive. Each of them was aware of the fact of ingrained human differences in tastes, dispositions and the like – 'second nature' – that were not the products of a universal human 'first nature'. But the term 'second nature' underscores a crucial point. The effects of custom mimic those of nature. So the effects of second nature can be identified only by subtracting the effects of first nature. This is a complex causal inference – not the sort that can be performed by simple inferences from behavioural measures.

Other older uses raise other problems. The problem of the relation between practices and explicit principles turns up in Berkeley, who comments in passing that 'two ways there are of learning a language, either by rule or by practice'.[9] This suggests that the two are or can be equivalent. Hume provided the most significant and startling use of the thought when he gave 'custom' or 'habit' as the explanation of the making of causal inferences. Hume's argument is worth recounting, because it is a model for later uses of 'practices' as ersatz principles.

Hume pointed out that inferring causal connections is something we do routinely. The inferences give rise to strong beliefs. The example he gives is our belief in the causal power of bread to nourish. The fact that, in the past, bread nourished me suffices to convince me that it will in the future. But the principles that might form the basis of the inferences are curiously weak. If we ask what principles justify the inferences, we get answers like 'the future will be like the past' – statements that are questionable or simply false. Our assent to them is far weaker than our assent to 'bread will nourish tomorrow'. Hume concludes that there is no principle that warrants such an inference. The explanation of the fact that we make these inferences is to be found not in traditional philosophical first principles, but in a fact of the natural world, namely the fact that children acquire the habit of making these inferences.[10]

Hume rather strangely calls this a 'custom' as well as a 'habit' – 'strangely' because for us the motivation for calling it a custom would be to draw attention to diversity, and this is evidently not Hume's point, for causal inference, though it may vary in some respects, is universal. But Hume is making another point – that this habit or custom resembles other habits and customs in their mode of acquisition and action. The habit of inferring causes is itself a cause of belief, and it is a cause like other habits and customs. But it is capable of playing a role like that of principles. Habits and principles, in short, might, as Berkeley suggests in relation to grammar, be substituted for one another. But in this case, Hume argues, the substitution can go only one way. Using the term 'custom' is a way of saying something less than this, something less than giving a justification, and something different in character. Hume says that if there is no possibility of substituting another principle for the habit, or providing some sort of analysis into simpler truths, 'we must rest with it as the ultimate principle'.[11]

The intersubstitutablity of practices or habits and principles is a given for Hume. Ordinarily, principles are better. In this case, he concludes, no principle can be found which does the explanatory work of habit – which explains the strength of our causal convictions. This is the form of the present philosophical use of the concept of practices. Today, however, one might reverse Hume's preference for principles, or hold that even if they were available they could do no more than articulate the practices that are the true foundation of our beliefs. One might say that the preference for accounts of belief in terms of practices is based on a recognition that 'first principles' do not explain anything, as we formerly thought they did, because there are no principles that are historically invariant with respect to persuasiveness – simply because persuasion always causally depends upon the hearer's possession of practices that may vary. But this kind of reasoning locates the concepts of practices squarely in the causal world, and this returns us to a familiar question. Are claims about practices, as Hume supposes, claims with causal implications? And if so, what is the causal structure of practices?

The term I have used here is 'practices', the plural. A more common term is 'practice'. The distinction between the two is important, but confusing. Here the history of the philosophical uses of the concept is more illuminating. Kant is the proximate source of the confusion, but the problem is with the term 'practice' itself, which bears both meanings. Kant wrote an essay on the saying 'this may be true in theory but does not apply to practice'. He explained this use of the term 'practice' with a remark that a practice may be defined as an activity seeking a goal 'which is conceived as a result of following certain general principles of procedure'. Sewing or medicine are 'practices' in this sense – at least one might try to construct a theory or a list of the general principles of procedure governing them. The issue, for Kant, was this. He conceded that there was often a systematic discrepancy between this 'theory' and the activity. But he thought that the apparent inadequacies of theory in the face of practice represented failures in formulations of the 'theory'.[12] With a correctly formulated theory, all that would be needed was the judgement to apply the principles to particular cases. Later writers disputed this. Some held that there was something to a practice, such as medicine, that was not reducible to 'theory plus the judgement necessary to apply the theory to cases'. At the root of the Marxian notion of praxis is something similar – that there is a living activity, with its own inherent goals, that cannot be captured in principles and procedures or reduced to theory. In this book I shall have little to say, except in passing, about this telic notion of practice. But it too leaves us with some questions. To what extent does a practice in the telic sense require 'practices' in the sense of ingrained habits or bits of tacit knowledge? To the extent that it does, the discussion of this latter sense is pertinent.

'Practices' today

We can close this brief family history of the concept of practices, as family histories can often be closed, with a sense of the inevitability of the present. The elements of the conventional wisdom of the present are visible in the faces of the past. The situation is simply explained. In postfoundationalist writings in the humanities, the diversity of human practices has become a place-holder or filler in the slot formerly occupied by the traditional 'foundationalist' notions of truth, validity and interpretive correctness. Truth, validity and correctness are held to be *practice-relative* rather than *practice-justifying* notions. Where we used to say that our practices, for example in science, were justified by the fact that they led us to truth, now we can see that truth is only that which our practices of representation enable us to construct as true. The radical results of postmodernism flow from this reversal. If practices are diverse and therefore 'local', then truth and validity are themselves local, and only local, because they are always relative to practices that are themselves local. If 'local' means something like 'shared within a network or group of people who have some personal contacts with one another' we can say 'social' instead of 'local'. The truths we can construct within our practices are thus 'socially constructed' – constructed by relying on practices that are themselves shared within a particular social group or network.

This reasoning leads, for those schooled in the philosophical tradition, to a series of perplexities. Is there anything that can validate our practices, our framework? Is the quest for some such validation a metaphysical itch that will go away in future generations? Or are we faced in scholarship with the situation of polytheism that Weber said we were faced with in the world of values? Is self-denying relativism inevitable – the fate of those who have eaten of the tree of knowledge, as Weber put it? But there is another possibility – that the picture itself may be defective. Finding a defect in the picture would not necessarily restore the idea of philosophical first principles. But it might open up other possibilities of formulation.

The key to the picture is substitutability. The traditional philosophy of first principles held that principles are supposed to rest on other principles – until we get to first principles, which were supposed to be self-evident and not in need of grounding. But if we recognize that there can be no such principles, that no theory can ground itself, we are faced with few options. What Hume called 'customs' (and I have been calling 'practices') are intersubstitutable with principles. They are not 'first principles' but they are in a sense better because they are more 'first' than principles. In the case of causal inference, for example, we are looking for principles to justify and explain something we already do. So the practices are 'first'. 'Intersubstitutability' is perhaps a misleading term for this, in one sense. We only seem to 'substitute' practices for grounding principles. In fact, the attempt to provide grounding principles by traditional philosophers is an attempt to substitute something explicit and universal for practices. To accept that these practices are the only 'ground' is to accept something that is already there.

The second element is the diversity of practices. Diversity is a fact that no traditional philosopher denied, but the fact was interpreted differently. Traditional philosophy thought we could justify our own practices by uniquely valid principles, and consequently could dismiss the practices of others as error. If we cannot – if even the validity of the principles we accept is relative to our practices of truth-establishing, and these practices could be different – we are compelled to be relativists, at least with respect to questions about the validity of practices. The only validity available to us is validity within our practices, or relative to them. This is a corrosive realization only when our practices rest on the illusion that they are more than practices. But knowledge-producing practices typically do rest on this illusion.

The diversity of practices is crucial in another way. It rules out most of the other options for replacing principles. Quine supposed that the naturalization of epistemology would involve the replacement of traditional epistemological principles by assertions of neurophysiology. But if the practices that are essential to the production of scientific results are part of historically variable local scientific cultures, neurophysiology, which is presumably neutral between scientific cultures, is not going to enable us to account for these practices, however useful it might be in accounting for vision, optical illusions, and the like.

Accounting for the diversity of knowledge, and certainly accounting for the diversity of morals, seems to demand some notion of practices. When we model the cognitive processes of a lawyer applying a code to a case, or explain the conduct of the senatorial families of Rome, we are faced with the same problem. The written procedures or laws, together with universal 'reason' and universal human motives are insufficient to account for what we know lawyers do and senators did. In each case we employ the same strategy to remedy this insufficiency – we appeal to the notion of special practices distinctive to each domain.

What separates us from the Romans is not merely the rules, criteria, means of assessment and the like which they employed and we do not, but the skills necessary to apply all these in the Romans' way. Both these skills and the criteria and principles are constitutive of the Roman way. They are what make the Romans' sense of the world different from our own. Our powers of persuasion and explanation, it seems, stop at the borders of our own localities. It is our *shared practices* that enable us to be persuaded and persuade, to be explainers, or to justify and have the justifications accepted. But the same justifications would not be accepted for a Roman, and thus there is no universal touchstone to which we could both refer either our disputes or our failures of mutual understanding. The same holds for the law. The point of legal training is to inculcate skills, skills that enable a lawyer to understand and formulate legal reasons and distinctions.

But this reasoning lands us right back to the world of the classical social theorists and their puzzles about causality. The fact that the ordinarily tacit part of legal reasoning can be modelled, with some success, in artificial intelligence programs indicates the problem. The concept of practice is not merely a useful term of interpretive art. It has the same ambiguities as the terms used by artificial intelligence: it describes an object-like thing with causal powers and a role in the world of cause.[13]

Rethinking 'practices'

The idea of practice relativity is powerful. The picture of knowledge as irremediably 'local' is compelling. 'Conventions without conveners' is a striking phrase. 'Tacit knowledge', 'spectacles behind the eyes', and similar phrases, such as 'inherited background' and 'tacit picture of the world' are similarly compelling, and no one was more compelled than I by them. But taken together their effect is numbing. Each of them is a name for an analogical object: something like spectacles, but 'behind the eyes', with the effect of conventions but without explicit agreement, like knowledge in some ways, unlike knowledge in that it cannot be articulated. Are these analogies the best that can be done? Are all these analogical constructions about the same basic stuff? If so, what is it? Or is it a mistake to ask these questions at all? Do we get any meaningful answers? Or is the concept merely a kind of aid to understanding? These questions have led me to conclude that the concept of practices is deeply flawed. My aim in this book is to give an account of the concept and its uses. But it is an account that will undermine the notion of practices, and especially in the form of the theory that practices are embedded in some sort of social substrate – the 'social theory of practices' of the title. This is not what I originally intended to do. But the results are as interesting as a constructive analysis of the concept would have been.

Hume could appeal to custom as a substitute for philosophical principles because he already possessed a concept of custom. The concept was borrowed from the public domain, so to speak, to describe the stuff of habit that he thought governed causal inference. We are in a parallel situation with practices. The concept of practices has a previously established use, indeed several uses. In this book I have chosen to explore uses in the tradition of social theory. The same argument, I suspect, could be constructed in terms of the uses in linguistics of 'presupposition', or by considering the general problem of artificial intelligence and the modelling of specific knowledge domains, or by examining 'constructivism' in the social studies of science. In each of these areas, and perhaps others, the employment of the term or its conceptual kin is sufficiently developed that the problems discussed in the book can be adequately exhibited. But social theory provides a more convenient starting point for several reasons: the issue of diversity is easily understood, the problems of causality easily formulated, and the variety of historically influential viewpoints is large.

In Chapters 2 and 3 I shall show first how the concept functions and identify the difficulties that are created by the standard ways of using it. In Chapter 2 I examine the 'causal' aspect of the concept, or rather the causal side of the family, and show why it ran into difficulties over identifying practices as well as in explaining them. Chapter 3 is concerned with 'shared presuppositions' and their kin. Identifying presuppositions turns out to involve a bit of circular reasoning. The circularity is essential to such enterprises as conversational analysis and ethnomethodology as well as Burckhardtian attempts to identify historical world-views. Despite the impressive evidentiary base of these enterprises, they still leave open the possibility that the 'presuppostions' they claim are 'shared' are not psychological possessions of those who are supposed to be sharing them.

In Chapter 4 I consider some highly general constraints on the notion of 'possession', showing that these standard usages cannot be reconciled with some minimal requirements of a concept of practice as some sort 'shared possession'. This discussion takes a simple form. The major constraint on any account of practice is what I call the problem of transmission (which in keeping with the 'possession' metaphor might better be called 'conveyance'). I shall show that no available model of practice adequately meets this constraint. What I believe I have done in

Chapter 4 is to develop an argument for the causal ludicrousness of the concept of shared practices and its many variants. The 'argument from causal ludicrousness' is not my invention, though the term is. What I mean by it here is simple. The concept of shared practices – the 'social theory of practices' – requires that practices be transmitted from person to person. But no account of the acquisition of practices that makes sense causally supports the idea that the same internal thing, the same practice, is reproduced in another person. Every causal account which attempts to establish sameness leads to ludicrous results.

The alternative is a highly familiar one. It is the notion of habit, a concept implicit in the concept of practices and its cognates. I shall conclude by sketching out an account of the inseparability of habituation from human activity and comprehension – an account through which many of the explanatory purposes that the concept of practice formerly served can be better served. This account, however, does not depend on the idea that 'practices' are shared or social, and consequently is not a 'social theory of practice'. It does not appeal to object-like shared entities. My point will not be to show that this alternative cannot be challenged on any grounds, but merely to show that it cannot be challenged on the grounds of existing concepts of practice. Its superiority, therefore, is relative to the concept of practice as it is commonly used in social theory and in the humanities. But this is superiority enough. The basis for the claim that practices exist is 'inference to the best explanation'. What I shall show is that there is a better explanation.

In Chapter 5 I consider the major uses of the concept of tradition and its variants, and ask whether the conclusions of Chapter 4 can be reconciled with them. The chapter is concerned with the problem of persistence, and the apparent conflict between an account of practices that denies the transindividual transmission of practices and the idea that practices can persist.

The arguments of the first five chapters are negative. In Chapter 6 I sketch out a picture that is consistent with the arguments, and deal with such issues as the concept of power, relativism and rationality. I have not, however, tried to show *in extenso* the implications of this argument. They extend, I believe, far beyond social theory. The idea of shared practices is an element of linguistics, artificial intelligence reconstructions of the mind, and virtually every available philosophical theory of interpretation, account of conceptual change in science and discussion of relativism. Much of the work done by 'shared practices' in these enterprises can be done by 'habits' – but not, I think without changes in the enterprises themselves.

2
Practices as Causes

> ... the actual government is not the result of a plan. It has arisen insensibly from the past states of the country, and has been adapted insensibly to its present situation. There are, moreover, important parts of the system which have arisen from usage and not from positive institution; and, owing to the subtlety of their operation as well as to the obscurity of their origin and growth, it is difficult to appreciate their origin or even to apprehend them accurately.[1]

The author is John Austin. The subject of this lapse from his usual clarity is the unwritten British constitution. What is he trying to say? What are the 'important parts' of the system that have these mysterious properties – obscure in origin and growth, subtle in operation and arising 'from usage'? Austin does not call them practices, and indeed does not name them. But he does describe several dispositions, and their effects.

The 'harmonious action' of the branches of Parliament, for example, is said to depend on the 'talent for compromise'. Austin takes this talent to be essential to both society and government, and claims that it was possessed in a unique degree by the people of England. The talent is produced by habituation. The relevant habits, the habits which produce the talent, include habits of character, such as habitual reverence for the rights of others and habitual moderation. These habits are found and reproduced in a certain class: they 'have mainly arisen from the breeding of the men who have formed the great majority of the lower house'.[2] The same habits are deficient in the lower orders, or so he thought, and this was the basis for his opposition to reforms that would extend the franchise.

Habit is something in the causal world, bound up in various causal relations. The process of habituation is a causal one, a process of individual psychology. Habits are individual possessions. But Austin is concerned with something with a history that goes beyond individuals. The habit of moderation on which harmonious action depends begins in the distant past and might end in the near future. He characterizes the history of the habit of moderation in a particular way, using a particular 'organic' vocabulary, the language of growth and adaptation, that is distinct from the vocabulary used for the individual fact of habit. The 'operations' of the thing itself are obscure; the adaptations are insensible. Presumably this means that if we compare at points of time that are sufficiently separate, change may be detectable. But the subtlety of the operation of this thing may defeat us.

Practices and habits

Austin is simply an example: the obscure thing Austin is pointing to figures in the writings of many others, and is a staple of nineteenth-century social theory. His account contains the basic elements of the concept of practice in what we may call its causal form. The structure appears repeatedly. The causal structure is tricky, for there are two parts to it: habituation, the individual part; and the part that goes beyond individuals, the historical part. There are two ways of thinking about the part that goes beyond individuals. Either a practice is an object with causal properties, powers of adaptation and the like, or it is solely a descriptive term, used to identify a set of things with a common feature, such as repeated acts exhibiting the quality of political moderation, which has no causal powers or structure of its own. Substitutes for the term 'practice', such as 'rule', 'norm' or 'tradition', occupy an ambiguous position between the two. 'Habit' is a convenient generic term for the individual causal fact; a convenient term for the historical fact that goes beyond individuals is less easily found.

'Habit' is itself a term with its own share of problems, and a troubled history. The ordinary uses of the term have fairly complicated causal implications. The term describes an activity, such as rising before dawn, which is an observable repetitive form of behaviour. But merely repetitive behaviour is not necessarily habitual: a distinctive mental component is required. This mental component is a cause, and claims about it are a matter of causal inference from its observable manifestations. Calling something a habit distinguishes it from manifestations with other supposed causal antecedents, such as impulses, reasons or instincts.

In view of the murkiness of these causes, and of the obloquy which behaviourism visited on mental concepts, it is worth recalling that the basis of the appeal of the concept was its considerable predictive power. In many cases, the observable manifestations of 'habit' are simple, and describing the pattern of behaviour will suffice to justify predictions. But the behaviourists, who dislodged habit from its centrality in social and psychological thought in the first third of this century, made an important point about habits when they derided the term for its appeal to unobservable mental entities.[3] 'Habit' is a hybrid term, at once mentalistic and observational. The difference between habits and repetitive behaviours, or the distinction between habit and innate inclination or impulsive act, is an aetiological one. To have a habit is to have a particular kind of mental cause operating. But the difference, the fact of the existence of a particular causal push that distinguishes a pattern of repetitive manifestations from a habit, is puzzling. Minimally, it is a cause different from the causes of impulsive or innate behaviour. Habits are acquired, and there is something which persists between manifestations, a mental trace.

To some extent, this picture can be fitted into a behaviourist framework. The time it takes to 'condition' a response can be measured, and the effects of various variables on rates of conditioning and on the rates at which a response is 'extinguished', can be studied experimentally, on pigeons as well as people. In this way the process may be demystified. But a number of problems re-emerge as soon as the demystified concept is applied outside the laboratory, to the 'natural' non-experimental facts which habit might explain.

One problem is crucial. Facts different in kind from habit, but having the same causal structure, of a causal force which we can identify only by inference from its effects, may be the correct causal explanation of a great many other observable manifestations or of the observable manifestations we might, in particular cases, explain by habit. My own habit of rising early, for example, might be the product not of habit but of circadian rhythms that are the effect of purely biological internal causes. Or my rising early on a particular day may have been the result not of habit but of a bothersome gnat.

The same kind of reasoning that we grant in the case of habits with directly visible manifestations, that there is an invisible 'mental' element by virtue of which the visible pattern of behaviour persists, may be extended to those 'habits of mind', that we can identify and speak of only indirectly, through complex inferences. These might include the habits of moderation or character discussed by Austin, or the habits of mind of modern science discussed by the pragmatists.[4] There is no reason to believe that there cannot be such habits of mind. The unobservability of the events or mental states they directly cause does not tell against their existence.

But the causal features of the concept of habit make it epistemically troublesome nevertheless. It is extremely difficult to make inferences about them. A person who 'habitually' rises early may fail to do so after a night on the town. But we are prepared to accept that there are conditions in which a habit may fail to produce the manifestation. With directly observable patterns of behaviour, we can more readily get a grip on exceptions and their occasions. In the case of habits of mind, these inferences about patterns must be made at one remove or more, for the patterns are themselves supposed to be mental, so they are accordingly even more difficult to infer. But there is no reason to suppose that the aspects and manifestations of the habits of mind that are most visible, and that we can make reasonable inferences about the existence and content of, are the whole of a person's habits of mind. Moreover, if it is generally difficult to make inferences about habits, and some habits of mind are more readily inferred from what a person says and does, there is no reason to suppose that there are not many more habits of mind that cannot be readily inferred but which operate nevertheless.

The difficulties of inference discussed so far are difficulties in inferring causes from manifestations. They arise because what is apparently the same kind of manifestation may have different causes. The same problem over causation arises for practices, or for habits of mind which are common to a group.

One reason the term 'habits of mind' has a Victorian air is that the boundary it was principally used to mark was the boundary with innate moral ideas or intuitions. In the struggle between utilitarianism and intuitionism, it was the thesis of the intuitionists that moral knowledge was interior and intuitively knowable. One version of this thesis held that this was placed within all persons by God: 'Written on our hearts, by the finger of their great Author, in broad and indelible characters'.[5]

The utilitarians were ridiculed by intuitionists on various grounds, mostly having to do with the character of moral experience: calculation of the sort upon which utilitarian judgements of goodness were held ultimately to rest, for example, is alien to moral experience. But the best argument for intuitionism was that it could account for something important to Victorian moral experience, which utilitarianism could not: the sense that people had of the evil of pleasures which were not harmful, such as sexual pleasure. One famous intuitionist, W.E.H. Lecky, rated 'chastity' as one of the seven things intuitively known to be good, and treated this intuition as a refutation of utilitarianism.

18   *Practices as Causes*

The utilitarians had answers to these objections. One of the places in which the notion of habits of mind was deployed was in these answers. The same phenomenological facts cited by the utilitarians, such as the unreflective abhorrence of the unchaste, could be accounted for by the associationistic theory of learning together with the idea that associations and sentiments persist after the original, explicit reasons are forgotten. Austin himself gave such an account:

> If I believe (no matter why) that acts of a class or description are enjoined or forbidden by the Deity, a moral sentiment or feeling (a sentiment or feeling of approbation or disapprobation) is inseparably connected in my mind with the thought or conception of such acts. And by this I am urged to do or restrained from doing, such acts, although I advert not to the reason in which my belief originated, nor recall the divine rule which I have inferred from that reason.[6]

This is a case of the habitualization of sentiment originally based on explicit belief. Austin used similar causal reasoning to account for our aversion to theft:

> Through my previous habits of thought and my education, a sentiment of aversion has become associated in my mind with the thought or conception of a theft: And, without adverting to the reasons which have convinced me that thefts are pernicious, or without adverting to the rule which I have inferred from their pernicious tendency, I am determined by that ready emotion to keep my fingers from your purse.[7]

If the language is archaic, the problems are not. Causal reconstructions like this are highly persuasive. The bits of the causal processes that are supposed to produce the aversion to theft are familiar and unproblematic.

The problem with these reconstructions is that the causal processes that produce the aversion are not independently accessible or observable. So in the crucial contest between explanations, the argument comes down to something other than fact, namely the consideration that there is no good alternative to the supposition that the aversion is acquired in this way. The argument is a matter of inference to the best explanation. But the merits of the competing explanations are often difficult to sort out. The inscription imagery, in which the hand of God writes morals on the heart, depends on a theology we no longer accept. So it is not a viable alternative. But other cases present alternatives that cannot be so easily dismissed. The reasoning in these disputes depends on arguments about what explanatory *desiderata* are most important in these contexts.

Empirical evidence can be made to bear on these issues, but it does so indirectly. Austin's associationistic account of the habitualization of morals was persuasive in this case because it had proved itself as an account of other phenomena. Related manifestations or indirect effects may fit one hypothesis better than another. Hume, for example, argues that childish errors about causal relations, errors that are later outgrown, show that the inferences are acquired through habituation. Chomsky's account of language-learning argues that the pace at which grammatical competence develops is greater than would be expected if the learning was the sort studied by behaviourist psychologists: children show 'anomalous precocity' in learning grammar. But as these examples suggest, the effects in question are very indirect indeed. Consequently the likelihood is great that persuasive alternatives to a given detailed account of the causal process can be constructed.

Berkeley's point, that knowledge of a language may be acquired either by learning rules or by practice, suggests another problem which will prove to be even more important. The 'same' overt behaviour in two people may have a quite different causal ancestry in each person. Indeed, one might suppose that habits that make it possible for a speaker to be fluent in a language may be acquired in quite different ways, that the underlying mental habits themselves are not 'the same' for different speakers, or that one or another of the rules that have been learned have been learned differently, so that the list of 'exceptions' that have been mastered is also different. This kind of causal ancestry fits Quine's image of bushes which have grown differently but which are trimmed to look the same.[8]

Constituting practices: the Mauss problem

For something to be characterized as a practice in the historical sense, the sense that goes beyond individuals, there must be some sort of sameness or identity between the practice at different stages. Austin's vocabulary of growth and adaptation works only if the same thing is growing and adapting. Yet Austin is not applying this language to an object that comes pre-constituted to us, as a natural kind. The hidden

20 Practices as Causes

parts of the constitution, on the contrary, are facts that we ordinarily would not notice as facts. 'Habitual moderation', for example, is by present lights a strange characterization of a political class.

Austin understands this, and says a great deal that serves to make 'moderation' into a distinctive fact. He describes the lack of moderation among the political classes of France: the 'contemptuous' bearing of the nobility towards their inferiors, and the response of the middle classes – 'burning hatred' for the nobility and a desire to 'return humiliation in kind'.[9] He also appeals to the fact that he had resided in France and Germany and thus was better prepared to appreciate the British constitution.

Austin's descriptive language is the language of object-like things – things that grow organically and behave causally. Habitual moderation and other sentiments play a crucial causal role in the preservation of the constitution. But the description 'habit of moderation' is vague, and does not seem suited to its causal status. The only way Austin can make it less vague, for the habit to seem to be a distinctive fact at all, is to appeal to comparisons to other political cultures. These appeals, however, depend on special knowledge, which Austin shares with his audience, about other societies, and about the immoderacy of their political classes.

It is not strange that one might not notice a fact or recognize its causal importance until one made a comparison. But something else seems to be at stake here. Austin's language was perhaps comprehensible to his contemporaries. But there is nothing that, for us, corresponds unambiguously to 'habitual moderation'. So we can better appreciate that Austin's characterization of the fact in question was not simply a matter of noticing a fact. Constructing 'habitual moderation' as a fact depended on the availability of specific comparisons, and on an audience to whom the comparisons made sense. We, today, are not such an audience, though we may grasp in a vague way what he thought. And this raises a deep question. Does the discovery of a practice depend on who the discoverer is? And if so, is there a fundamental conflict here? Practices, understood as object-like things, should be the same for all who seek to identify them. Are the things we call practices in fact the same for all who seek them?

Marcel Mauss, the nephew and student of Durkheim, provides the classic case of the discovery of a practice in his essay on techniques of the body.[10] In this essay he recalls lying ill in a hospital in New York:

> I wondered where previously I had seen girls walking as my nurses walked. I had time to think about it. At last I realized that it was at the cinema.

Returning to France, I noticed how common the gait was, especially in Paris. The girls were French and they too were walking in this way. In fact, American walking fashions had begun to arrive here, thanks to the cinema.[11]

The elements of the situation may be specified in more detail. Mauss had some sort of unarticulated expectations about how women walk. Then he noticed a difference – but not merely an idiosyncratic walk, which might have had an aetiological origin in a physical anomaly, or simply have reflected the random distribution of individual differences in walks. He was able to match the social distribution of this unexpected gait with categories that he already possessed, such as 'American', 'at the cinema', 'after his return to France' and 'in Paris'. He realized that he had previously encountered the gait of his American nurses at the cinema, and this fact supplied him with a causal hypothesis: that this fashion had arrived in France through American films. He does not tell us how this process of arrival worked, but we may suppose that it worked something like this: impressionable girls unconsciously imitated the demeanor of American actresses in the films and thus altered their gait, and the change became habitual. Perhaps it was then unconsciously imitated by others.

Mauss could distinguish the walk as habit *because* he could say that the difference in walks he had noticed was not a natural difference, and he could say that it was not a natural difference because he could give a historical account of it. He started, so to speak, within a culture with its expectations. In what sense, however, is this starting point within a culture necessary? Could one start from nature? Or alternatively, could one 'naturalize' descriptions of practice that are first constructed within a culture in terms of difference with descriptions that are culture-free?

Any attempt at constructing a culture-free description of a practice must face the problem discussed in Chapter 1 in connection with Cicero's slogan, 'custom is second nature'. How does one distinguish first, or human, nature and second nature, or practice. Consider the case of a Martian observing the walks of earthlings. The Martian might, like Mauss, have formed certain expectations through observing French women which could have been confounded when he continued his observations in New York, or on French girls. But he would, as a Martian, have had no culturally given expectations. All earthlings' conduct would be, for the Martian, natural. The reason for this is simple. The distinction between first and second nature is aetiological. Human

22 Practices as Causes

nature is a cause. Showing that some external pattern of behaviour, such as a manner of walking, varies between cultures or between social categories suggests rather strongly that the difference is learned – that the cause is not in human nature, or that human nature is implausible as a cause. A Martian biologist might arrive at explanations which were based on a naturalistic account of this same causal ancestry and arrive at distinctions that correspond to the 'cultural' distinctions made by Mauss between French and American girls. But to do so, the Martian would have to have access to the mental machinery by which the behaviour is produced in order to distinguish biological or mechanical causes from psychological causes, such as habit.

Arriving at culture-free causal categories that correspond even roughly to the differences observed by Mauss presents formidable difficulties, even for a Martian. An exterior performance, such as a manner of walking, is the result of the composition of many causes – body properties, shoes, training and setting. The 'same' external walk can be produced by various combinations of causes. One might acquire the 'same' walk by mimicking or by a kind of training which corrected various untutored walks — and corrected them in different respects – to produce a walk which is externally the same. By beginning with causes, as the Martian must, one is faced with massive complexity. The Martian could overcome this complexity if a relatively short list of basic human mechanisms or codes for storing the mental trace that is the causal element of the habit was discovered, such that each actual habit would correspond to the encoded mental traces. Alternatively, if the modes of acquisition happened to fall into a set of natural kinds that could be causally connected with the behavioural performance of the habit, habits could be identified and correlated with these causes.

If either of these strategies served to substantially reduce the causal complexity faced by the Martian, and the Martian produced causal categories that more or less corresponded to Mauss', it would then be possible to ask whether the Martian's causal explanations were explanations of Mauss' fact about the differences in the technique of walking, or the explanation only of the facts described in the Martian's vocabulary. There seem to be two kinds of cases in which we would accept the Martian's explanations and accept his categories of description. One would be where we recognize the decisive superiority of the new categories of description and abandon the old categories. The second would be to match anomalies: to show that when we treat something as exceptional on one level, such as an irrational act, there are anomalies at the level of the biological descriptions claimed to correspond to it, such as neurochemical imbalances that correspond to patterns of irrational behaviour. If the anomalies in the behaviour correspond, more or less, to anomalies in neurochemistry, we can accept the rule of correspondence for the normal case.

There seems to be no reason in principle why the project of matching up or replacing exterior, cultural descriptions and interior biological descriptions cannot succeed, and it is plausible that it will succeed in some cases. A researcher has recently claimed to have evidence of the existence of a grammar gene – a heritable flaw in the capacity to speak grammatically.[12] If true, the description 'congenitally ungrammatical' might replace other descriptions, such as 'ignorant', for people with the flaw. But the idea that the whole of 'cultural' variation, or even a large part, could be matched up to biological variation would require a scientific miracle.

To say this is not to say that there are no biological influences on culture, that culture can be understood without reference to the causal facts of biology, or that there are no biologically based human commonalities that are part of the causal background to particular practices. On the contrary, all these theses are probably true. It is simply to say that, at present and for any foreseeable future, there are not going to be correspondences between biological descriptions and 'cultural' descriptions that are useful in distinguishing practices from one another, or in distinguishing first and second nature. And this means that there is going to be no path to an 'objective' description of practices through biology – through matching up culturally rooted descriptions of practice to 'culture-free' biological descriptions.

Another kind of objectivity might be sought *through* cultural descriptions of practices. Return to the example of Mauss. The identification of a pattern of girls' ways of walking depended on Mauss' starting point: his expectations, unconsciously formed, of how girls walk, which the American gait violated. What he noticed as 'the American walk' was what contrasted to the way of walking with which he was familiar. Yet Mauss himself wrote as though a general kind of description of these cases was possible. He suggested constructing a worldwide inventory of body techniques, which would require at least a general set of boxes into which differences could be classified. But he never constructed such a scheme. What he did instead was to give examples of differences. In the case of walking, his examples are such differences as walking with the hands open or in a fist. The differences, taken together, would yield a classification scheme, but one which is

24 *Practices as Causes*

simply the product of the contingent fact that these differences were known to, or recognized by, Mauss.

In the case of very simple differences, such as the difference between walking with a closed or open fist, it can be explained and understood by members of any human culture. But 'the American gait' or 'habitual moderation' cannot be dealt with so easily. They do not lose their dependence on the contrast with unarticulated expectations with which they conflict. And these unarticulated expectations are 'cultural' and local. Mauss and Austin, like their heirs, are tempted to objectify practices. But they cannot: practices are objects of a peculiar kind, dependent on a cultural perspective.

Durkheim's nightmare

The systematic mismatch between practices as they might be causally explained and practices as they are discovered and conceptualized by people with unarticulated 'cultural' expectations, between practices as a part of the world of cause and practices as they came to be revealed, was experienced in different ways at different points in the history of social thought. Durkheim experienced it as a conflict between the vocabulary of social description, which he characterized as 'ideological' and that he knew derived from religious doctrine and similar sources, and the vocabulary of explanation – the vocabulary needed to explain the fact that traditions, moral ideas, customs and the like had a stability beyond individuals, and that they behaved in certain respects like causal objects and were the source of causal forces that acted on the individual. The idea of customs as things and of these things as the sources of causal powers acting on the individual, led to the idea that 'society' was the source and locus of these causes. This idea commended itself as a solution to one of the chief conundrums of late nineteenth-century social thought. If God or human nature was not the source of moral feeling, and if moral feelings varied significantly from society to society, why not say that the source of moral feelings was *in* society, and that 'society' needed only to be properly understood as a novel causal order?

The influence of this solution, which appeared in various forms, was enormous. But the problem of arriving at a proper understanding of society as a novel causal order was insurmountable. Durkheim thought that it could be solved by conceiving of society as analogous to an individual mind, and discovering the laws of the collective mind, thus establishing it as a causal order. Tönnies sought to show that different societies produced different social 'wills', and that the social will was experienced by the individual as a moral commandment. Both of them were influenced by a philosopher of law, Ihering, who, like Austin, had been influenced by Bentham but was compelled by the problem of the causal power of norms to go beyond utilitarianism. Ihering's solution was to say that there is a collective interest that overrides individual interests.

Durkheim's project of explaining the elements of the social mind analogue, the collective consciousness, was a failure: with a great deal of trimming, he was able to 'explain' a few aggregate patterns by reference to law-like underlying principles. To make these explanations credible, he would have had to continue the programme, and he could not. But the various late nineteenth-century attempts to make explanatory sense out of practices had some important consequences. The practices and representations of a society came to be seen as a kind of ensemble which could be understood only in relation to one another. The kind of understanding these ensembles lent themselves to was teleological and holist: the body of practices as a whole, the structure, did the adapting, or the functioning. The pattern of slow growth and adaptation which Austin found in parts of the unwritten constitution was transferred to a different level: society as a whole. The practices of a society, accordingly, came to be seen as 'social' in the strong sense of serving the deeper purposes of society, operating together with the other practices of a society.

The reasons for this development may be appreciated if we consider the causal concept of practice that had the greatest influence on social thought and subsequently on public discourse in the United States, the concept of the *mores* articulated by William Graham Sumner. The *mores*, Sumner wrote,

> are the ways of doing things which are current in a society to satisfy human needs and desires, together with the faiths, notions, codes and standards of well living which inhere in those ways having a genetic connection with them. By virtue of the latter element the *mores* are traits in the specific character of a society or a period. They pervade and control the ways of thinking in all the exigencies of life, returning from the world of abstractions to the world of action, to give guidance with revivification.[13]

Sumner gives the *mores*, 'this vast system of usages', some peculiar causal traits, which result from the particular kinds of facts he takes to be indicative of the influence of the *mores*. Mauss had been impressed by such things as the shape of bakers' shop-windows in different parts of France, which he took as an indication of the boundaries of Celtic influence. Sumner emphasized the tyranny of the *mores* as irrational routines which become obligatory, the limitations and triviality of the free choices open to people, and the unconscious and unreflective character of the *mores*.

What distinguishes such a conception from utilitarianism is this. The *mores* are not the product of reflection and conscious selection, but are the product of a kind of social experimentation that began in primitive ignorance and fear and was partially blinded, not only by the inability of humans acting collectively to, so to speak, process the feedback from these experiments, but by the omnipresent element of risk, which, together with ignorance, makes collective experimentation desirable only under pressure, such as the pressure of changed external conditions which change fundamental interests. The defects of collective rationality which characterize the situation in which the *mores* were established are obviously irremediable – at least from the starting point of primitive ignorance. The primitive person would not comprehend the solutions. So what evolves through the blind experimentation of history are habitual patterns, deviation from which is sometimes punished by nature and is always bounded by unknown risks.

How the habits that result from repetitive attempts 'to live well under existing conditions' as Sumner says, became 'coercive',[14] and came to be seen as good, as right, and to have the status of facts, was a puzzle that was never satisfactorily solved. If one starts with habits and they are understood solely as individual psychological facts, it is difficult to see how these become something else, such as a moral obligation shared by others. The solutions to this problem vary. If one allows for some sort of collective decision-making in which moral authority is granted to a lawgiver, the laws given can become habitual, or the habits of individuals can be altered by the actions of the lawgiver.[15] This was Weber's solution, or one of them.[16] Another was to suppose that there was an innate, biologically based revulsion against change, such as the change represented by the deviant. The genealogy of morals could then be inverted and an alternative model of morals created.[17] The primal situation could be reconstructed as one of solidarity, sameness and fear of innovation rather than one of struggle between Hobbesian individuals. Individualism could be accounted for as a by-product of the breakdown of primal solidarity.

Each of these various histories was bound up with different core concepts of their subject matter. Different concepts required that different causal questions be answered historically: to give a causal history of *mores* was to give a history of deep underlying causes; to give a history of morals as habitualized ideology was to give an account of the prophets and leaders who established the ideologies. But the historical answers were not, in the end, terribly convincing. No causal concept of morals won out, and the project itself withered. Today it is the domain of sociobiologists and other amateurs. Sociologists and anthropologists took the easier route of giving 'functional analyses'. But the basic point made by Sumner and his peers was not lost. The idea that cultural differences were stable, deep, and largely impervious to manipulation was central to the functionalist picture of society.

So Durkheim's nightmare came to pass: in the case of culture we recognize ourselves to be in the presence of powerful causal forces that we are powerless to grasp conceptually in causal terms. Cultural differences came to be thought of in ways that owed little to these elaborate historical and causal theories. Knowledge of cultural difference was valuable as a means to understanding. The task of understanding was, implicitly, a task of translation, and for this instrumental task, the Maussian problem, the problem of the cultural relativity of descriptions of cultures, was irrelevant. The aim of understanding was best served by user-friendly descriptions, descriptions that relied on terms with a familiar meaning within European culture and thought, such as 'convention' and 'presupposition,' and 'culture' itself. It is to these usages I now turn.

3
Practices as Presuppositions

> The tacit conventions on which the understanding of everyday language depends are enormously complicated.[1]

Mores are unmistakably causal things; values are not. Values may be simply objects of thought. But values are often treated as causes. And they are often at the same time treated as presuppositions that are tacit or not consciously 'thought' about. Indeed, the tacit sense of 'value' is bound up with the causal sense, because to attribute a tacit value to a person one must point to its effects on the person's conduct. The term norm works in a similar way. Norms, in the sociologist's sense, are identifiable only by observing what happens if they are breached. The economist's term 'preference' is similar as well. Preferences are attributed by causal inference from behaviour. So these terms still have a foot in the world of cause.

The 'presuppositions' analogy

The concepts of preference and norm seem to solve the problem of vagueness that afflicts *mores*, Durkheim's underlying social facts and other such causal concepts of practices. Norms can be treated as causes, yet specified with precision, unlike *mores*. The terms are terms with an established place in discourse, in explicit reasoning. Indeed, we make inferences about a person's preferences, purposes, values and norms more or less routinely in common-sense contexts, and act on these preferences, as when we see that Aunt Millie always prefers chocolate to lemon pie, or is particular about how familiar she is with delivery men. We can often articulate the rule of preference we infer quite precisely. Aunt Millie may be able to do so as well. And we may even engage her in a discussion of the subject and reveal her preferences to her.

The same holds for 'presuppositions'. Terms like 'presuppose', 'premise' and 'assume' – terms from logic which have a specific meaning in the context of explicit logical proof – are used analogically to speak of our own and others' reasoning or action. These terms are open to an extension popularized by Kant's late nineteenth-century successors, the 'new' Kantians, who had learned the lesson of the historical diversity of intellectual forms. Their use of 'presuppositions' to mean tacit premisses – an equally mysterious notion – survived as a cognitive or quasi-cognitive surrogate for the naturalistic terms habit and custom. And it not only survived. Together with such concepts as ideology, structures of knowledge, *Weltanschauungen* and a host of other similar usages, the idea that there is something cognitive or quasi-cognitive that is 'behind' or prior to that which is explicit and publicly uttered that is implicit and unuttered became the common currency of sociologists of knowledge, historians of ideas, political theorists, anthropologists and others.

The term, 'presupposition', where it is used to describe a 'background assumption' (that is, a claim that is neither explicitly formulated nor consciously adopted by a reasoner), works by a cognitive or linguistic analogy that is very similar to the way 'preference' works. One shows that a person 'presupposes' something by showing that, if one or more of the person's beliefs were made the conclusion of an explicit logical argument, premisses in addition to those explicitly avowed by the reasoner would be required to make the argument valid. One shows that a person draws conclusions as if they were reasoning from these premisses, and infers that the possession of these tacit premisses was the cause of their beliefs.

This is a modest-looking step with very large implications. To be sure, presuppositions that are initially outside explicit reasoning can at least sometimes be formulated explicitly and added to the list of explicit beliefs to which a person assents. But in itself this establishes little about 'presupposition' as a psychological fact, a possession of a person.[2]

Identifying presuppositions

At first glance, the concept of presuppositions seems more powerful than the causal conception of practices. One needs only to hold an argument or belief up to the strict standards of logic, and thus to the standard of completeness and explicitness in justificatory reasoning, and the presuppositions (the tacit premisses) will be identifiable by the gaps in the reasoning of the premisses needed to make the argument (the explicit argument as reconstructed) valid. But this kind of reconstruction, as we have seen, has an unwarranted premiss, the analogical principle that the reconstruction matches some sort of inner mental reality.

Extending the individual psychological application of the notion of presupposition to the social case, to account for shared practices, involves another problematic analogical step. If we grant that 'assumptions' may often be 'made explicit' – or at least statements can be constructed to serve as substitutes for particular individual dispositions in particular reconstructions of explicit logical arguments – it appears that, sometimes at least, practices may be treated as presuppositions (as Kant does in the case of Hume's 'custom' of causal inference). This raises the tantalizing question of whether customs, or at least those of philosophical interest, may all be ultimately reducible to, or formulable as, explicit statements. If public agreement to various 'conclusions' is the starting point of analysis, and some argument can be made explicit which warrants these common conclusions, and premisses of these arguments can be analogically imputed to those who agree with the public conclusions, the problem of the commonality of the premisses between individuals disappears, and one can speak of *mentalités*, tacit ideologies, world-views and the like as autonomous objects, ready for historical explanation or at least for the question of who in time and space had these presuppositions. But if the analogy breaks down, the issues become more complex.

One problem that arises immediately is underdetermination. The same conclusions may be drawn from arguments with different premisses, and there is no reason to believe that a given formulation of the 'presupposition' is either the only one possible or the one that corresponds uniquely to the psychological reality of the person to whom the presupposition is attributed. The testimony of the individual is of no help here, save perhaps in excluding attributions by showing them to be inconsistent with other explicit beliefs.[3] But inconsistencies in belief are not psychologically impossible (though perhaps one could redefine the key terms, such as 'belief', in such a way that it is impossible by definition). Kant himself had his troubles with this: there was more than one set of premisses sufficient to warrant the same spatial reasoning about physical objects. Kant dealt with this problem in a manner which is not entirely satisfactory from the point of view of the psychology of the matter: he rejected the existing alternatives to his own favoured conceptions on grounds having to do with their philosophical adequacy. But there is no reason to suppose that the psychologically or historically effective presuppositions will be the philosophically preferable ones. Indeed, if one believes that humanity begins in error and improves its 'assumptions', one believes that erroneous 'assumptions' were once psychologically effective.

There is an even more crucial problem. If there are several possible sets of presuppositions that suffice to fill the logical gaps and supply the necessary premisses for some publicly assented to set of beliefs, then there is no reason to believe that the same set is psychologically effective within all the individuals who assent to the public beliefs in question. Different people often have different reasons for assenting to something in public; there is no reason to suppose that they do not have different 'presuppositions' as well.

So underdetermination makes 'sharing' questionable. This kind of problem might be resolved on causalist grounds by arguing that it is causally improbable that the members of a common culture have somehow had implanted in them different presuppositions. Same processes of implantation, same presuppositions, is a plausible causal rule. But if the presupposition picture is collapsed into the causal one in this way, all the problems of indirectness of inference that produced problems of vagueness return. Our evidence with respect to hidden processes of implantation is nil.

When we move to the level of collective or shared presuppositions, we encounter some analogous problems. To understand how they arise, we need to return to the basic use of the concept of 'presupposition' as an explanation. To 'explain' a belief by reference to its presuppositions is to identify hidden or tacit beliefs that justify it; only reasons or beliefs justify other reasons or beliefs. The appeal of the 'presuppositions' picture itself rests on this. The justification of a given belief is another belief that warrants it. In the case where people appear to believe something for no reason, the belief is explained analogically by a hidden belief, a tacit belief or presupposition that would justify the belief.

There is an obvious support for this reasoning in the practice of supplying 'assumptions' for others and gaining their assent. If we are lost on the road, and I notice that the landmarks are passing in the reverse order from what we expect, I may say, 'We assumed we were travelling north, but we aren't.' In these prosaic cases it appears that we can uncover what is there but simply unacknowledged, namely our assumption. And we may often get easy assent on our attributions of assumptions: 'That must be right – somehow we got turned around.' It is an easy step from playing this kind of language game to thinking of the 'assumption' as a piece of our psychological history, as something that we, in a hidden act of 'assumption' put in our minds and can now disassume.

But to come to see that we are reasoning as if we believe something is sometimes not so simple or immediate. One needs, for example, to become cognizant of modern economic theory to come to see that one's ideas of fairness in pricing 'assume' a particular economic conception, namely the medieval just-price theory. Something similar to this is the normal case in science: to understand the 'assumptions' of previous scientific theories, one needs to have an understanding of new theories to which the past theory may be compared. In these cases, the starting point is the new theory or theories, and the presuppositions are identified differentially – premises that vary are supplied in place of premises in the new theory in order to produce the different explicit conclusions of the past theory. In general, indeed, we discover our own assumptions, to the extent that we do, by standing on the stern of our boat and watching for them in the wake, and finding that they become easier to identify the farther they recede.

There is no direct access to these presuppositions, in the sense that one could, for example, engage in a Socratic dialogue or an inner reflexive dialogue which would induce, say, the adherent of the medieval theory of prices to verbalize the 'assumptions' of the theory – not, at least, unless the Socratic questioner or reflecting person was cognizant of the alternative theory. Clever adherents to the just-price theory might, if they knew some modern logic but no modern economics, respond to demands for definitions of key terms, such as 'just-price', by saying that these were simply the primitive terms in the only possible theory of the phenomena of economic life. But they could not be induced to verbalize the premises that differ from modern economics unless they were given the alternative – that is to say, taught modern economics, or were able to invent a simulacrum of it on their own.

In cases like that of the travellers who assumed they were going north, it seems that access to assumptions is immediate, and there is no 'comparison'. So the idea that this assumption is a psychological reality is more plausible. But in this case there is more. The travellers can consider causal facts, such as getting turned around, and they can without difficulty, indeed immediately, conceive of the alternative assumption, and then check its differential implications. The travellers are not verbalizing something unusual, still less something that had never before been verbalized, such as the concept of directionality; rather, they represent a case of providing an explanation citing a belief of a kind that is routinely verbalized: 'We are going north.' Even where the specific verbalization is a novelty, it may be understood as an exercise of a familiar, learned capacity for salvaging sense in a situation by supplying alternative assumptions. This can be done for other persons as well as for oneself, so here there is no implication of special access to one's own 'assumptions'.

The reasoning in the case of the travellers can be decomposed into some of its elements. First there is some sort of perplexity in word or deed which suggests error or at least variation between people in thinking about something. One can explain this by identifying 'premises' that account for the difference. There is a small element of the psychological or causal in this. Something needs to be causally effective to make the words or deeds into intentional action as opposed to behaviour with no cognitive content. But causal facts otherwise do nothing to discredit 'assumption' attributions. The sole test of an attribution of assumption is its consistency with other beliefs attributed to a person and its ability to solve the explanatory problems that are presented by the act – the error or misunderstanding which produced the need for the attribution of an assumption.

In the case of the travellers, the starting point is error, that is to say, something that can be recognized and overcome without learning any new presuppositions. In the case of the just-price economic thinker, the difference with the modern economist cannot be overcome – at least by the just-price thinking – in this way. New 'presuppositions' – or a new way of thinking – must be learned. The possibility of misunderstanding, and the form the misunderstanding can take, is limited by the starting point of the parties to the misunderstanding. The travellers have the same starting point; the economists have different starting points.

In these cases, then, the Maussian problem simply arises in a novel form. The assumptions the modern economist attributes to the just-price thinker are identifiable as assumptions only because the modern economist is in a position to make a specific comparison such that the reasoning of the just-price thinker can be reconstructed and explained by attributing certain pre-modern economic assumptions. Starting from a different comparison – between the just-price theory and the economic thinking of Kwakiutl participants in potlatch exchange, for example – would produce different misunderstandings, and different assumptions would need to be attributed in order to overcome the misunderstanding and account for the explicit beliefs and deeds of the parties to the comparison. Such 'assumptions', then, are not natural facts, but hypotheses that solve specific comparative problems.

In the case of practices conceived causally, there was a gap between the 'practices' that could be constructed on the basis of specific comparisons (between the French and American walk, for example) and the causal facts that the practice (the walk, in this case) consists of. 'Presuppositions' turn out to raise the same problem, at least when the concept is applied to cross-cultural cases.

Burckhardt's problem

In Burckhardt's famous studies of, as Patrick Gardiner puts it, 'the vision of life underlying the relics left by former times',[4] the 'vision of life' is attributed on the basis of the relics. Some visions of life are consistent with the relics, and others are not. Those that are not can be eliminated on the grounds that persons with the wrong vision presumably could not have left the relics in question. The existence of relics, however, does not establish the claim that there was in fact a shared vision of life. The idea of shared collective presuppositions, as we saw in the last section, was a convenient analogical extension of the idea of 'presupposition' from its psychological application. But we earlier saw that the psychological application, the conclusion that the particular premises that would make the utterances of a person into valid reasoning are in fact among the tacit psychological possessions of that person, was unwarranted – it is simply a hypothesis, and other hypotheses might be true. The extension to collective beliefs is doubly problematic, for it rests on the attribution of presuppositions to individuals and the attribution of the same presuppositions to everyone in the collectivity.

The reasoning behind the extension to the collective case is this: people share certain explicit beliefs or activities. These explicit beliefs or activities would be possible only if they also shared certain tacit beliefs; hence they do share these tacit beliefs, and the tacit beliefs are causes of the behaviour in question. The phrase 'possible only if' in this formulation masks a complex problem. The 'possibility' in question is not simply the logical possibility of affirming a given explicit belief. Reciting the Nicean Creed is a case of explicit affirmation of belief, but no one supposes that everyone who does so means the same thing by it, or that everyone who recites it 'believes' it. So the kind of 'possibility' in question is different and not terribly clear. The relationship is not, as

Practices as Presuppositions 35

with assumptions like 'we're going north', between explicit beliefs or actions and tacit premises that would make the reasoning valid, but between a novel kind of object and a novel kind of collective mental fact. In Burckhardt's case, the novel object is the set of relics and the novel collective fact is the 'vision' of an age.

The difficulty with these arguments is parallel to the problem of the individual psychological reality of 'presuppositions'. The existence of the relics is treated as evidence for the existence of an underlying vision. Perhaps the hypothesis is the best explanation – but the evidence used to select between alternative 'vision' hypotheses does not serve to undermine the 'no shared vision' hypothesis. The same problem arises for other cases of collective *explanans* for collective *explananda*.

How is this problem solved? One tactic is familiar from Durkheim: to characterize the objects of the explanation as a distinctive, hard and independent universal order of facts that can be plausibly accounted for in no other way than by the collective mental object hypothesis. Durkheim pointed to anomalous or unexpected regularities, such as the relation between the *couvade* and the avunculate, that held cross-culturally, where no order was expected. Durkheim's version of this 'universalizing' argument failed because he could never get beyond making a few isolated cross-cultural facts conform to a law-like pattern. *Le Suicide* was his only 'success'.

But similar tactics have been used to establish the factuality or autonomy of collective cultural facts within specific cultural orders. Foucault and the members of the *Annales* school engage in a kind of description of unexpected patterns in past cultural practice. In the case of Foucault, these are often shocking images or events, which are then placed into a coherent pattern. In the case of the Annalistes, typically some domain of practical conduct, such as conduct relating to odours, is shown to have a long and coherent history of its own. In both cases the specific puzzling practice or occurrence is transformed into an element of a pattern with its own independent facticity. There is revealed to the reader a structured, public, shared set of actions or signifiers that can be analysed by identifying 'deeper' or at least simpler rules of structure or categories of thought that in turn can be attributed to the individuals who perform and interpret the signifying acts, and located in their mental world.

By shifting the 'order' from the explanation to the thing explained, it is made to seem that only a collective fact of some sort – some shared mentality – can explain the order. But this strategy runs into its own form

36 Practices as Presuppositions

of the Maussian problem. Establishing the reality of practices by pointing to unanticipated orderliness is itself dependent on the prior expectations of the reader, which are violated, and is relative to these expectations.

We are sensitive now to Burckhardt's selectivity and his dependence on his own cultural starting point because so many alternatives have subsequently been constructed. Each takes different facts as the hard stuff that points to the shared mental structures, and each comes to different conclusions about what the shared mental structures are. And we can see that many of these accounts, including Burckhardt's, depend on the following kind of inference: if we produced these objects or engaged in these activities, we would have to believe, value or think about the world in such and such way, hence they, our historical subjects, thought about the world in that way. The starting point, meaning the relics taken as puzzling, different and therefore problematic, as well as the solution, are relative to a particular historico-cultural starting point.

Recognizing this dependence on a particular historico-cultural starting point opens up a possible solution to the problem of circularity. We can simply accept that the constitution of these objects, and the explanatory solution, is relative to the starting point of the inquirer who is a member of a community with its own shared tacit rules. We can concede that the inquirer can 'construct' the tacit rules of another community only by a process of discovering that something done by the members of this other community is done differently or in an unexpected way. The failure of her or his expectations – expectations which are products of the inquirer's own experiences conditioned by the shared rules of her or his own community – is a *prima facie* indication that the practices of the community or local setting being studied differ. She or he can then hypothesize a practice that fits the behaviour of the members of this community, including the puzzling behaviour. This would be an 'as if' rule only: it would say that, in the case of the problematic expectation-confounding behaviour disclosed to the inquirer, the members of this community or local setting behave as if they follow such and such a role or employ such and such a technique. This hypothesis may compete with other hypotheses and the conflicts between alternative 'practice' hypotheses may be impossible to settle, but ordinarily they can be settled by further observation, because the practice hypothesis warrants predictions.

So far, the inquirer is constituting the practice. The practice may then be 'explained' by showing it to be a variant of our own practices (as such exotic practices as lustral rites may be seen as a variation of baptism) and by showing how we would have to think (what tacit rules we would have to follow, and so on) in order for us to fit in with the behaviour of the community being studied and to mimic its members' responses. The comparison enables us to identify our practices by the contrast between our behaviour and theirs. We might come to discover that it is not 'natural' for adolescents to go through years of anxiety and unhappiness before becoming adults, and infer that there is something in our practices of age categorization, our sexual taboos or other practices that accounts for this difference. These practices come to be seen as practices, as part of the cultural rather than the natural world, through these contrasts, and only through such contrasts.

What I have just outlined is an unashamedly relativistic approach to practice. It concedes that what is revealed about our practices is a matter of the contingencies of available comparisons, and that a 'practice' as such, practice as an object, is inaccessible. 'Practice' here is used instrumentally, rather than to denote a real thing, either a causal object or a 'presupposition' lodged in the mind. The inquirer can be simply agnostic about the reality of practices. The term itself, used in connection with this kind of explanatory project, is simply a useful way of talking about the instrument we use. The problems it is used to solve are questions of how one makes sense of people's sayings and doings in order to engage in interaction with them in a wide range of practical intellectual contexts. The puzzles or problems arise through failures of interaction, in which our expectations are revealed to have misled us. The origins of the problems are practical, but situational or relative, not theoretical.

This solution to the problem of explaining practices preserves the instrumental value of Burckhardtian accounts – that is to say, their value for us as means of understanding past eras or other cultures. But it leaves out something crucial. The issue is difficult to get a clear view of, but the common metaphorical usages are suggestive. Bourdieu's phrase, 'inscribed on the body', captures the problem quite precisely: the need is to connect the stuff of thought to the world of cause and substance. The predictive use of either the concept of practice or the 'psychological' concept of presupposition and its variants depends on the idea that there is some substance to it, something with more continuity than the words or acts which exhibit the practice or presuppositions. The instrumental uses of the concept itself seem also to require some sort of substance and continuity beyond the overt manifestations. Unless we can proceed as if a practice were real, a cause that persisted, we would have no basis for using our past understandings or interpretations to warrant future

38 *Practices as Presuppositions*

interpretations. Moreover, if practices are in some sense causal and persistent, they ought to be potential subjects of causal explanations, not just translations, comparisons and interpretations.

Making practices into things

Considerations of this sort lend support to attempts to construct a concept of practice along the lines of Durkheim: to identify some hard factual stuff that corresponds to practice, and to construct a theory of practice by inference to the best explanation of that stuff. The general difficulties facing this strategy have already been hinted at. The first is that nothing about the existence of some set of shared public objects – Burckhardt's 'relics', for example – in itself entails the existence of a shared mental structure in terms of which people understood these objects. The second is the proliferation of explanatory objects. The fact that each new wave of historiography or analysis finds or constructs different 'hard facts' to explain feeds the suspicion of circularity; it also presents the problem of reconciling the various practices and presuppositions that can be attributed on the basis of these differently selected and constructed 'facts'. The third is the Maussian problem. To what extent does the selection and construction of facts depend on particular historico-cultural starting points? If dependence is inescapable, as it seems to be in the case of Burckhardt or the historians of *mentalités* of the *Annales* school, we are faced with a major problem.

The most interesting recent formulations of this idea have been in the context of discussions of practices of representation or the social construction of facts.[5] Accounts of fact-making practices raise issues of reflexivity. Aren't facts about practice just 'made' facts as well? If so, isn't the story that social constructionists tell itself just another story about the facts being 'made' by scientists, law courts and the like – and not the 'true' story?

The origin of the problem in this form is in sociology, and is connected to the fact that the study of fact-making in sociology was originally motivated, at least in part, by an attempt by ethnomethodologists to provide a critique of the attempts of conventional sociologists to treat such things as questionnaire responses as hard facts. Their criticism of ordinary sociological analysis was that sociologists appropriated folk categories that were themselves practices of objectification and representation. These practices had the effect of mundanifying or banalizing bits of the world, making them unproblematic or given, and consequently creating a naturalistic illusion about facts that were really constructed. What ought to happen, according to these ethnomethodologists, is that the practices should themselves be the subject of study, that they be topics for analysis rather than resources. But certain ethnomethodologists, such as Cicourel and Pollner, saw that the criticisms that they had levelled against conventional sociological analysis could be levelled back at them.

One conclusion that might be drawn from this 'reflexive' consideration is that to talk about practices, even to identify and describe them, requires representing them, objectifying them or 'mundanifying' them, and that consequently the idea of a standpoint external to, transcending, or better than mundane reason is illusory. Other ethnomethodologists rejected this, claiming to have discovered, or to have procedures that reveal, a realm of facts that have, once revealed, special properties that mark them out as facts. Their reasoning, *in nuce*, is this: what is revealed is orderliness, which is 'local' or socially situated (meaning exhibited in the doing of 'members'). Members become members by learning the orderliness. So the 'teachable–learnable' properties of the orderliness signal the existence of practices – practices are taught and learned. The facts of orderliness are thus explained by the existence of particular practices.

In its naïve form, this reasoning is subject to the same criticism levelled against Burckhardt in the last section. A passage from the writings of Harvey Sacks, one of the founders of conversational analysis, provides a simple example of the argument. Sacks thought that one could exhibit some generative principles for the production of what he calls 'possible descriptions'. He gave the example of two sentences from a story told by a nine-year-old girl: 'The baby cried. The mommy picked it up.' The sentences are heard, so he claims, as: 'The *baby's* mommy picked the baby up.'[6] Sacks concludes that the fact that almost everyone who hears these sentences draws these conclusions shows the facticity of culture. It gives us

> ...some sense right off of the fine power of culture. It does not, so to speak, merely fill brains in roughly the same way, it fills them so that they are alike in fine detail. The sentences we are considering are all rather minor, and yet all of you, or many of you, hear just what I said you heard, and many of us are quite unacquainted with each other. I am, then, dealing with something real and something finely powerful.[7]

The language Sacks uses here – the business about culture 'filling brains' not 'roughly in the same way' but 'alike in fine detail' – is not representative of either Sacks or conversational analysis. But it is explicit where other formulations are evasive. It shows exactly where a certain leap in this reasoning occurs: between the fact that is taken as evidence of a common possession (of 'members' in the jargon of ethnomethodology) and the characterization of the common possession itself.

Sacks' depiction of brains being filled by the same stuff, 'alike in fine detail', is what philosophers call a 'picture', not an argument. But it is a picture that raises some important questions. What exactly is at stake in the distinction between filling brains 'in roughly the same way' and 'so that they are alike in fine detail'? Is this merely a rhetorical flourish? Or does the whole project of analysing presuppositions hinge on some notion of 'sameness'? And if so, what is the same, and where, if not in brains, is it? The constraints on answers to these questions will be the subject of the next two chapters. Here it will suffice to note that the problem takes many forms, but each requires a similar leap: from an object of explanation which is understood to be in some sense shared, such as a phenomenon of mutual order, to an explanation in terms of something that is also held in common.

A more current version of this leap would dispense with the 'in the brain' picture, and replace it by the following: 'Sacks attempts to address an array of commonplace "techniques" that we use ubiquitously, but which do not readily come to mind when we reflect upon our language and linguistic capacities.' The techniques are not 'in the brain' but 'are embedded in the routines they produce, and are "recalled" for analytic inspection by reproducing (replaying, transcribing) the dense singular details of conversation'. Locating the techniques 'in the routines they produce' has a crucial advantage over Sacks' naïve formulation: there is no puzzling physical, causal gap between the object of explanation and the thing which explains. The only access to these embedded techniques is through 'carefully unpacking the orderly composition of the discursive objects that embody them'.[8]

One difficulty with this is that the distance between the explanation and the thing explained disappears. The thing described, the phenomenon of order, is so closely bound to the things that explain, the techniques, that we may begin to doubt that we have an explanation at all. We have no independent access to them, because they are embedded in the phenomenon.

This is a problem for Burckhardt as well: our access to the world-vision of the Renaissance, after all, is only through relics, including, of course, literary relics. The techniques, the common possession and use of which does the explaining, are coextensive with the phenomenon of order, and evidence for the one is evidence for the other. Describing order becomes the focus for research. The order identified cannot be explained other than through 'embeddedness'. The teachable–learnable techniques are embedded in the routines that produce order. The reason 'techniques' can be taken to explain, however, rather than merely describe, is that the teachable and learnable stuff – whatever it is – is not merely embedded in the thing described. It must also be in people, because people do the teaching and learning, in the form of a capacity or possession of some kind that enables someone to perform. So there is a difference, and this difference makes the one into an explanation and the other into an object of explanation. But it is idle to inquire into the question of what is in people's brains and whether it is really alike in fine detail, because our only evidence that it is there at all is the evidence of its teachability and learnability, evidence which comes from our observations of the order itself and which shows it to be teachable and learnable or shows teaching and learning as part of the order.[9]

This solution is neat, but it is just a bit too neat. The difficulty is this. The fact of learnability and teachability is crucial to the explanation. The evidence of 'order' is intricate, precise and descriptive and (as in the case of Burckhardt's relics) new evidence can help decide between alternative 'collective-possession' hypotheses. But the evidence relating to learnability and teachability is indirect, and allows for alternative non-collective explanations. The difficulty may be seen through Sacks' own distinction between filling brains in 'roughly the same way' and in ways that are identical down to fine detail. The evidence of learning and teaching, such as it is, takes one form: it shows that someone may acquire the capacity to perform as a member through interaction with others already performing in this way. This is Berkeley's learning by practice. The evidence about what is learned is no more than the evidence of successful performance.

Sacks assumes that the intricacy of the order implies the commonality of what is learned: the shared rules which produce this intricacy. The evidence, however, establishes only that the ability to perform well enough to be taken to be a member can be acquired through practice. The teachable–learnable character of the ability implies that it is a causal fact – in some sense, something is in someone's brain, in order for them to perform on the basis of this acquisition. But it is an open question as to what is indicated by the fact that the performances are sufficiently congruent for the 'orderliness' in question. It might be that the causal stuff is the same down to the fine details, as Sacks' picture indicates. But it might be otherwise. It might be that the causal stuff, the capacities created through habituation or practice, are very diverse, and that different persons with their quite different habits can perform in ways that continue the orderliness in question.

The distinction between 'same enough in performance to continue the appearance of order' and 'alike in fine detail' is crucial, and applies to many formulations other than Sacks', so it needs to be carefully formulated. We need first to distinguish kinds of 'sameness', and ask what kind the evidence bears on. One kind we may call 'instrumental'. Instrumental sameness is sameness with respect to achieving a given purpose – such as performing in a way which continues the appearance of order, or producing grammatical sentences, or some other goal. Causal sameness is sameness with respect to the mechanisms that produce the performance. Evidence of instrumental sameness is not evidence of causal sameness. One can perform as if doing so in accordance with a given technique, for example, without one's performance being caused by one's acquisition of that technique.

We have no direct access to the causal mechanisms, so we cannot assess their sameness directly. Our indirect access to the causal mechanisms is typically by means that establish sameness with respect to performance. From sameness with respect to performance we might infer sameness of causal mechanisms. We can make this inference more plausible by describing the performances in such a way that alternative causal explanations become less plausible, and through reasoning that the fine-grained sameness of complex performances must require fine-grained sameness in causes. But the indirect evidence we have about habituation or learning by practice in general does not lend much support to this reasoning. Fine-grained complexity of mutual linguistic performances can be sustained between persons whose linguistic habits, whose uses of terms and whose responses to them are subtly and often not so subtly different, and whose history of acquisition varies widely. One would suppose, for example, that the differences between first- and second-language acquisition would be substantial with respect to the underlying causal structure of linguistic habit. But the performances may be indistinguishable, and the orderliness of the performances – for example of philosophy professors speaking a language which one of them has learned as a second language – may be impressive.

The elusiveness of practices

The argument of the last two chapters may be summarized very brutally. The concept of practice, whether it is conceived cognitively, as a kind of presupposition, or causally, as a kind of mental trace which disposes thought or action in a certain way, is epistemically elusive. Practices are not directly accessible, and the means of accessing them indirectly are fraught with difficulties, of which underdetermination is the most obvious and pervasive. The required inferences are inherently flawed. They do not distinguish between 'as if' explanations and causal explanations. They may establish that phenomena of order may be produced by people acting as if they are acting in accordance with certain shared procedures or rules, but this is not the same as showing that these (or any) shared procedures are the causes of the 'order'.

These epistemic quibbles in themselves do not disqualify the concept of practice from a prominent role in our thought, or indeed from the role it now plays, as a kind of opaque endpoint to reflection and explanation. But the epistemic problems have some non-epistemic implications. Practices, by any conception, must be transmitted. We are familiar enough with the transmission of information, sentences, texts and the like. In these cases the problems of transmission are more or less equivalent to the problems of knowing – knowing is, so to speak, successfully receiving a transmission of information. In the case of practices and presuppositions, however, matters are different. The practices of concern to enthnomethodology and conversational analysis, for example, are supposed to be embedded in routines, accessible to analysts only through feats of inference. Practices, in short, are hidden. These other things are not. How can these hidden objects be transmitted – is there, so to speak, a special orifice which receives them? It is to this question that I now turn.

4
Transmission

> It is clear that moral feelings are transmitted in this way: children observe in adults inclinations for and aversions to certain actions and, as born apes, *imitate* these inclinations and aversions.[1]

How do presuppositions or practices get *implanted*, if this is the right metaphor – how do they get to wherever they go in a person, and *where* do they go? How, also, are they *imparted*, or sent *from* this place, and in what form are they sent? Are they transmitted directly from individual to individual, for example by imitation (a favourite of Nietzsche and Tarde)? Or do they go through some medium, some sort of collective ether, such as 'the social' or 'discourse?' And if so, how does the practice get from the ether to the person?

The question with which the last chapter closed, of whether there was some special orifice through which practices arrived, was not wholly tongue in cheek. Questions about transmission point to a large and powerful constraint on any theory of practices. However one conceives practices, one must conceive them in a way which is consistent with at least the possibility of transmission, and the ways in which one conceives the possibility of transmission necessarily limits the kinds of conceptions of practice one may consistently adopt. This constraint is not, of course, purely a theoretical problem in the 'social sciences'. To appeal to the notion of practice in a philosophical argument, for example, one must suppose at least that the problem is soluble in principle, and soluble in a way which does not require a concept of practice which conflicts with the philosophical uses to which it is put.

The uses need to be kept in mind to forestall some apparently telling, but misleading, criticisms. One criticism would be that the argument presented here is itself no more than a case of the usual struggle against fictiveness, an attempt to privilege a form of description as 'matching reality'. But this objection is self-undermining. The point of calling something fictive is to say that it is, like a fiction, 'made'. The worlds we make through rhetorical practices are 'fictive' because they are made. Either the process of 'making' is real, or the process is a fiction. If 'worlds' are not 'made', there is no basis for calling them fictive. If the 'making' is real, the practices that are part of the making must be real as well. Explanations end someplace: these explanations end at practices. So what must 'practices' be?

The point of appealing to the concept of practices in these contexts is to provide a better endpoint to explanation, a substitute for 'reality', essences, or true meanings. All of these terms point to something 'outside' discourse. 'Practices' is a better explanatory backstop. Yet it is better not because practices are not 'real' or not 'outside', but because the concept enables us to account for differences between 'fictive' worlds. It fits with the phenomenon of the historicity of forms of thought and expression, with the apparent connections between social change and change in forms of thought, with the social distribution of forms of thought, and perhaps most importantly with the facts of acquisition through teaching, particularly the fact that practices appear to come along as baggage with the formal teaching of, for example, canonical texts. The substantive characteristics of practices, that they persist *in* the individual and beyond individuals, that they have some effect after the teaching is over, and that they are acquired in typified situations rather than innately, are precisely the characteristics that qualify them for this role as an 'outer', delimiting, substantive fact. To abandon this substantive character, which is, as I have shown in the previous two chapters, 'causal' in at least the minimal sense described above, is to lose the backstop, and put oneself in need of a substitute backstop.[2]

What is the issue? Defining the issues here in a generic way presents problems. Each conception of practice presents the problem in a different form. The core issue is perhaps this: if practices or presuppositions are hidden things, or tacit, how do these things move through channels that are themselves public or open? The concept of imitation, for example, works for public things, such as overt conduct. But unless the hidden thing can be converted into and out of overt conduct by the transmitter and the receptor, it cannot be conveyed. So a first pass at a formulation of the problem might be this. Some subset of material (text, information and so on) is considered to be unproblematically acquired by individuals or transmitted between them.

46 Transmission

The subset, or its process of transfer, however, is insufficient in itself. Something else must be acquired in order for the transfer of information or the reading of a text to take place. The innately given capacities of individuals are insufficient for the purpose of assimilating the unproblematic stuff. People are, so to speak, decoding and encoding boxes who are transferring material in coded form. So the procedures of encoding and decoding must also be transferred.

This is all rather abstract. The mundane facts that motivate this problem are these. We often cannot understand what other people mean other than by translation, which is to say by the conscious application of knowledge acquired in such familiar ways as teaching or from books. We often cannot understand what the behaviour, gestures and doings of other people mean other than by consciously inventing and then selecting on the basis of observations a hypothesis that explains this behaviour. But we know that the people we are attempting to understand did not themselves acquire their capacity to speak a language through formal teaching or books, or come to understand one another's gestures and performances by consciously constructing and testing hypotheses. So there must be some other way to acquire the capacities that we simulate or substitute for by our laborious conscious efforts. The puzzle is how they are acquired.

The epistemic problems about the identification of practices with which the last two chapters were concerned define this problem negatively: whatever else may be said about the transmission of practices, they cannot be transmitted through the ordinary epistemic routes, in the ways that knowledge is ordinarily acquired, at least as they are ordinarily conceived by epistemology. A practice is not a visible object, nor is it a linguistic object, such as a sentence. Our only access to it as inquirers is through inference, often of a very indirect kind, involving particular kinds of comparisons and subject to various restrictions. So our access to practices as *recipients* of practices, as acquirers of the tacit knowledge or culture that is 'shared' with some people and not shared with others, must be through other means.

It is ordinarily assumed that our employment of these other means of acquisition is not fully conscious, and that we do not have the same kind of access to our acquisition of tacit knowledge or practices as we have to other kinds of information. We can recall, for example, the minute when we heard that Kennedy was assassinated, but we cannot recall our acquisition of the capacity to speak a foreign language or do proofs in elementary logic. In the latter cases we seem instead to *discover* that we have learned to do these things more or less competently, or *conclude* that we have done so on the basis of our observations (and the observations of others) of our own performances. And as we may be simply unaware that we possess a practice, just as Mauss' *jeunes filles* did not realize they had a certain way of walking, we are necessarily also unaware in these cases that we ever acquired it, and therefore how, when, and from whom or what we acquired it.

There are, it seems, easy ways around this problem. The easiest is to say that of course there are observable regularities that can be explained in no other way than by *mores*, internalized norms, presuppositions, *mentalités* and the like. They have to go someplace, if they are to be 'internalized', so there has to be some mechanism for going there. The burden of proof is thus on arguments against the sufficiency of known mechanisms.

The 'known mechanisms', however, prove to be as elusive as the stuff they transmit. With transmission, we have all the epistemic problems of the last two chapters, and more besides. Transmission is known, as the practices are known, only indirectly, through inference. But since what is being transmitted is a hidden thing known only indirectly, a practice, we can adduce only two kinds of evidence. First, we may use the overt, observable performances as evidence of possession. We may, for convenience, call these the 'phenotypes'. The hidden causal things, the practices, we may call the 'genotypes'. What we can observe is the phenotypic fact of similar behaviour in another person. Second, we can also observe facts that are consistent with the acquisition of this genotypic stuff, such as contact with those who exhibit the practice, or participation in activities or training through which the dispositional patterns are transmitted or shaped.

With a little imagination, we can invent unconscious or inexplicit analogues to conscious and explicit forms of transmission, such as teaching or training, much in the same way that concepts such as 'presupposition' and *mores* were constructed in the first place. We can suggest that there is unconscious learning of tacit knowledge, or that there are unconscious versions of processes of acquisition with which we are familiar on the conscious level, such as discipline, and claim that they are central to the transmission of practices and sufficient to account for them. Or we can evade the issue by employing metaphors that shift the burden of explanation to others. To take a simple example of this, consider Bourdieu's concept of 'reproduction'. It suggests a process by which the patterned dispositions that, for Bourdieu, constitute the 'practice', the *habitus*, of a person or of the members of a group, are *duplicated* inside new people, such as the children of members of the group. But Bourdieu does not trouble to give a psychological account of how this might happen – he leaves that to the psychologists, or to the imaginations of his readers.

Shifting the burden of proof in this way is a wholly legitimate tactic, but only a promissory one – the promise is that the burden can, in principle, be shouldered, and that the solution will not undermine the concept of reproduction. By characterizing the transmission of practices in the way he does, Bourdieu creates a *prima facie* case that there is a phenomenon of reproductive transmission. If there is, accounting for it is a problem for psychology – for learning theory, perhaps. If learning theorists cannot account for this kind of learning it is a failure of learning theory, rather than a failure of Bourdieu's theory of practice. Thus his theory is extremely difficult to 'refute' in the ordinary way. But the same thing that makes it easy for Bourdieu, the fact that the transmission of a disposition must be inferred in two steps, from phenotypic similarity to genotypic similarity and then to the fact of transmission, makes it easy for the proposer of alternatives. And the competing model need only account for the observed manifestations, the phenotypic facts of the supposed process of reproduction, in other terms.

In assessing alternative accounts, however, we are stuck with a weak set of considerations. We can identify cases that are difficult to assimilate to the practice-reproduction model, and better fit some other model. But the practice-reproduction model, because of the indirectness of the inferences that sustain it, fits with all sorts of phenotypic facts. The next best consideration is one of simple plausibility. The psychological mechanisms of the transmission of dispositions are a bit odd. So this issue might serve to distinguish the models, and make one distinctly superior to the other.

If an alternative to 'reproduction' could be constructed in terms of psychological mechanisms that are already well established on other grounds, one would not need to cash in metaphors, however attractive (as 'reproduction' is), by matching them up with hitherto unknown or undiscovered psychological processes. Unfortunately, if the mechanisms of transmission cannot be those familiar from the epistemological tradition – seeing, sensing, the hearing of utterances of linguistic objects such as sentences and the like – we are at a loss. Our apparent alternatives are such dubieties as introjection and unconscious imitation. The list of alternatives might be improved on. But the fact that there is no unproblematic mechanism puts the question up for grabs.

Weak as these considerations are, they are not empty. Moreover, a great deal is at stake, at least potentially. It may be that a concept that appeared at first to be a great analytic convenience, and indeed was and continues to be, on fuller examination turns out to lead in directions and have implications that undermine the very categories it was initially employed to save. The idea of reason as a distinct, pure and universal capacity, for example, was undermined by the recognition of radical cultural diversity. The idea of a separate capacity of reason that was universal was salvaged by the claim that *within* the admittedly diverse cultural practices and presuppositions of various societies, reason is the same everywhere. If the idea of cultural practices and presuppositions that works best as a substantive idea undermines this solution, the idea of reason that was initially saved is up for grabs again.

Here again we need to remind ourselves of the reasons the concept of practice was appealed to in the first place. The concept is *not* an 'ordinary' concept, nor is it a philosophical one. It is, as 'custom' was for Hume, a concept from another domain. It was appealed to at a point at which ordinary language concepts failed, specifically at the point at which it was necessary to account for the fact that some people appeared to use different concepts and regarded their concepts as 'ordinary' as well. To avoid the problems with the concept one needs to avoid appealing to it, or to its kin – something that philosophy, along with a number of other disciplines, has found difficult to do. The reason for this is plain. The concept of practice cannot be treated as so much ideological baggage because it is being employed as the means to account for the phenomenon of ideological baggage itself.

Location

The considerations that we may bring to bear in assessing alternative accounts of practices and their transmission may be weak, but some are less weak than others. The least weak, indeed the *pons asinorum* of this whole tradition, is a problem in which various issues intersect: the problem of the *location* of practices. Location, the *where* that the transmission needs to get to, tells us what the task of transmission is. Locations also bear on powers. The causal properties attributed to the practice need to correspond to their location.

In Chapter 2 I noted that the concept of practice had a two-level

50   *Transmission*

structure – that it was both a concept that had to have some sort of *individual* substance and some sort of *historical* substance. Mauss' (and Bourdieu's) notion of *habitus*, to take a simple example, is both an individual fact – a matter of individual dispositions and the like – and a social and historical fact. *Habitus* come and go in history. They are or are not 'reproduced' in other people, to use Bourdieu's language.

This bi-level structure gives the theorist of practice three basic options in finding a 'location' for practices: Each option comes with its own distinctive transmission problems.

Collective-object solutions   They may be located in some sort of shared object, such as a text, or a 'social' substrate in which the shared practice exists. The transmission problem takes a familiar form: the individual relates to this common object by *interiorizing* or *introjecting* it, in the manner of a Parsonsian 'norm', or *grasping* it, as a Wittgensteinian rule or a principle of mathematics is grasped.[3] The 'transmission problem' is this: what do terms like 'interiorize' mean?

Private solutions   The individual mental trace in which practices persist, namely individual habits, may be understood as the true location of the practice. The public or overt manifestations of practice are understood as causal consequences of the existence of these habits. The transmission problem is with the supposed mutuality or commonality of a practice – the fact that it is 'shared' or comes to be shared. If the real things are habits, they are not common or shared. What, then, makes mutual understanding possible?

Dualistic solutions   The shared object has two faces or two types of causal powers. If it is some sort of dispositional entity, for example, it is simultaneously collectively shared within some group, and has some force as a group object, *and* is individual or private in its causal force and effects.

Dualistic solutions

The dualistic approach seems at first so *outré* that its appeal needs some explanation and illustration. Discussing it may appear to be a detour, but it is not. The three options are not as neatly distinguished in the literature as I have made them here. Many accounts, indeed, trade on ambiguities between options, particularly by solving the transmission problem by appealing to mechanisms that work only for different concepts of practice. Elements of dualism occur so frequently in the later accounts – the ethnomethodologists discussed in the last chapter are a contemporary example – that it is a good place to start.

Durkheim and Tönnies held views illustrative of dualism. In Durkheim the problem of the simultaneously collective and private character of practices and representations is solved by saying that practices and representations have causal power, that individual and collective practices and representations reside in the same place, the individual mind, but that collective practices and representations *also* reside in a collective consciousness, governed by its own laws. For Tönnies, the idea is that there is a collective intentional force, a kind of common social purpose, that is in potential conflict with individual purposes and interacts causally with them in the individual mind.

The motivation for these accounts as Hans Reichenbach puts it, is to 'explain the fact that moral volitions appear to us as secondary volitions, as the expression of an obligation'. He gave a standard dualist explanation, namely 'that these volitions are imposed upon us by the social group to which we belong, in other words, that they are originally group volitions'. The examples he gives are 'not to steal, not to kill and so forth'. The mark of dualism is the phrase 'in other words'. The two things – that volitions are 'imposed upon us' by the 'group' and that they are 'volitions' *of* the group (necessary for group preservation, as he says) are not the same. A 'group' can 'impose' volitions without 'group volition'. Reichenbach further muddles the issue by his description of the mechanisms of 'imposing' these group things which does not appeal to the notion of 'group' at all: 'As generations passed, individuals were conditioned to these rules; and in our own education we were subject to a conditioning process of the same kind.'[4]

> No wonder, then, that we feel ourselves on the receiving end of the moral imperatives; in fact we are. If a feeling of duty is regarded as characteristic for moral aims, such a conception mirrors the fact that moral aims were instilled into us forcibly, whether through the authority of the father or by the teacher or by the pressure of the group in which we lived.[5]

The contrast in descriptions of forms of transmission is worth noting, because it exemplifies the way in which the problem of transmission serves as a kind of litmus test. Reichenbach needs a process that corresponds to the lurid physical vocabulary of forcible instilling, pressure, receiving, imposing and so forth. And it is clear that the 'rules' that are being forced into people are a kind of collective thing, a 'group ethics'. But the only *mechanism* of transmission he identifies is 'conditioning' – unless he imagines that group pressure is a distinct path of causal influence.

Conditioning works through externals, and different experiences produce different results – though a form of education can be arranged, so that sameness of response, phenotypic similarity, is the result of the conditioning. This is not the same as forcibly instilling a collective object, such as a distinctive 'group ethic', based on collective purposes, into each member of the group.

The attraction of dualism is this. Dualism avoids the problem of the achievement of mutuality or 'sharing' by definition – the collective part of the mind, or whatever is taken to be collective, is 'mutual' by definition. It also avoids the problem of grasping or introjecting, since the mutual stuff is already there. There is a price – some kind of mechanism by which collective causal impulses develop and change must be identified, and the problem of the relations between the two parts of the mind must be resolved. In Durkheim the problem of introjection is made into a matter of mutual contact, and the collective part of the mind is said to be revived in special moments of collective unity, such as rituals. These moments may also be times in which collective mental change may take place.

Tönnies locates the collective element in a different place in the mind – in relation to habit and will. He argues that morals must be based on a group will or intention that is expressed in the mental world of individuals as a causal force, but is carried in the individual in the form of habit, habit produced by repetitive action in accordance with this *Wille*. His case for the existence of a group *Wille* is that it is an explanatory necessity – *Sitten* and their force, especially the individual's phenomenological sense that the demands of morals or custom are in conflict with the individual's own desires and that the individual is submitting to a higher demand, cannot be accounted for without reference to some kind of intentional 'force'. The form of argument should by now be familiar: the intentions in question, the demands of morality and the like, are explicable *only as* social purposes or goods, so the only possible conclusion is that there must be such collective purposes and intentions.

The problem faced by all dualistic solutions is to link the individual and collective aspects or elements. Tönnies collectivized purpose, and made collective purposes into individual causes, in the form of the force of habit. Durkheim collectivized cause directly, locating causal forces in the collective consciousness. Both then needed to flesh out, in a plausible way, the explanatory picture they presented. If by present lights they failed, it is a failure made visible to us largely as a consequence of the fact that the causal and purposive imagery they selected from contemporary science is now visibly archaic. Both Durkheim and Tönnies, for example, were captured by the rhetoric of 'social forces' and thus concerned with the source of the 'force' which brings about the causal results they attribute to 'the social'. This idea of forces – as a kind of liquid stuff – is a relic of a defunct scientific rhetoric.

Concealed forms of dualism: Fish as a Durkheimian

Present-day users of the concept of practice do not wear their commitments to these alternatives on their sleeves. On the contrary, evasion of commitments, especially on the subject of transmission, is the rule. Indeed, the character of the appeal to the concept of practice is often so vague that it is unclear which of these three locational options a given user has in mind, and as we shall see the three options tend to blur and run into each other in actual usage. To say that there is a *mentalité* or *Zeitgeist* that is characteristic of a given group or epoch is to *imply* something like what Durkheim and Tönnies say explicitly – namely, that 'the thing is a causal reality in individual minds and interacts causally with other causes' *and* that it has some kind of supra-individual substance or reality.

But the users of these locutions do not wish to commit themselves to the kinds of models of mind one finds in Durkheim or Tönnies. One reason is obvious. There is simply no evidence, other than the very indirect evidence of common patterns of overt behaviour, that there is a 'collective consciousness' or group *Wille*.[6] In itself, this should be no deterrent to the construction of such theories. The more serious difficulty lies elsewhere: the mechanisms by which they are supposed to operate are inconsistent with everything we know about causal processes in other domains. In the case of Durkheim and Tönnies we have come to this realization largely as a result of drastic changes in fashion in scientific rhetoric. And there is a lesson to be learned from this history. We should recognize our susceptibility to properly packaged variants of the same basic dualistic solutions. The packaging – which recently has taken the form of talk of DNA replication and computer viruses (a locution, one may note, that preserves the notion of reproduction) – will, we can

54 *Transmission*

expect, ultimately seem as ludicrous as the talk of 'currents' in Durkheim. But it is difficult to resist the packaging, especially if there is no alternative to the concepts of practice, and therefore no alternative to accepting transmission as a fact, however mysterious the explanations of this fact might be.

The literary critic Stanley Fish is a gold-mine of Durkheimian usages, all of which are probably unconscious – there is at least no evidence that Fish ever read a word of Durkheim. Fish replaces Durkheim's idea that society is made up of practices and representations which 'constrain' its members with the idea that 'interpretive communities are no more than sets of institutional practices'[7] or, elsewhere, 'beliefs and practices' that constrain its members.[8] The parallels go on. Durkheim supposed that individuals belonged to a variety of 'societies', such as the 'domestic society' created by a marriage; Fish supposes that individuals are members of a variety of interpretive communities whose constraints may conflict.[9] Durkheim stresses that the causal structure and constraining character of the causes located in the collective consciousness is not transparent and indeed is obscured by our everyday concepts. Fish says:

> However nuanced one's talk about constraint, belief and community may get to be, the nuances will never add up to a moment or place where consciousness becomes transparent to itself and can at last act freely. Being embedded means just that, being embedded *always*, and one does not escape embeddedness by acknowledging, as I do, that it is itself a fractured, fissured, volatile condition.[10]

Durkheim treats this 'fissured, volatile condition' as a peculiarly modern and abnormal one; Tönnies historicizes the 'condition' in the same way – the loss of *Gemeinschaft* and the emergence of *Gesellschaft* mean that the unity of collective intention is lost.

For Durkheim, the term for the setting in which one is 'embedded' is milieu: both are locational metaphors. Both Fish and Durkheim think about society or interpretive communities anthropomorphically. For Fish,

> The community is always engaged in doing work, the work of transforming the landscape into material for its own project; but the project is then itself transformed by the very work it does.[11]

More generally, he says, 'Practices are continually being transformed by the work that they do'.[12]

This is a typical Durkheimian inversion: society becomes the directing agent and the individual its subject. But Durkheim, eager to avoid simple teleology, proposed complex *causal* feedback mechanisms to produce the same results.[13] In Fish's hands the image of the community takes the naïve form that the community is a kind of agent with its own project or purposes. This is a notion more congenial to Tönnies' notions of collective purpose, and Fish does in fact appeal quite freely to the notion that activities have supra-individual purposes.

Fish discusses a piece of sociological research by D.L. Wieder dealing with 'the convict code' and the way in which the convicts operate in terms of a prison ethic (a 'code' which is displayed in their speech but which is not an explicit set of rules).[14] He characterizes the code – a term used by Wieder in a punning way to indicate both that it is a secret communication system among convicts and a moral standard – as an 'enterprise ... a moving project or bundle of interests', and as a 'general project whose implementation involves the continual discovery of its own content, a discovery that is at the same time the accomplishment of its own alteration'.[15] The code is treated by both Wieder and Fish as a substantial reality of its own. Where Wieder suggests that it be thought of as a 'process', Fish makes it into a kind of purposive being, but one which is at the same time an 'instrument for organizing contingent experience'.[16]

With Fish's 'instrument' language we come close to Foucault. We are presented with a novel kind of dualism, which preserves the idea of the code as a common purposive object, and, at the individual level, an instrument. Yet Foucault, more sensitive perhaps to the difficulties of the Durkheimian project, is more cautious about his commitments, and avoids the suggestion that 'projects' are substantially real, with its problematic consequences for location. The problem with collective purposes is that they need to be located in a collective place, such as a collective consciousness, which can be related systematically to individual consciousness. As Durkheim and Tönnies learned, this is difficult to do. Foucault avoids these problems, which arise with every dualistic solution to the problem of location, by incorporating the dualism directly into a novel object. Power/knowledge techniques are not instruments or collective purposes but collective means which subject their users. But these means need to be acquired, and in this respect the concept faces the same problems of transmission as other members of a large family of similar solutions.

56 *Transmission*

Collective-object solutions

The concept of 'rule' as used by the followers of Wittgenstein presents the transmission problems of the members of the family of solutions to which power/knowledge techniques belong in a simpler and more readily understood language. The idea of 'rule' follows a simple pattern we have noticed with other terms. The usage is based on an analogy to the common possession of a public object or to public agreement. 'Convention', which has a readily intelligible meaning in its public use as an explicitly accepted mutual agreement, becomes 'convention' in the analogical sense of a tacitly agreed to basis for mutual action or understanding – convention without conveners. Similarly for 'ideology': in the original sense of this invented term in the writings of Destutt de Tracy, an ideology is simply a right way of thinking, constructed as a guide to thought and formulable in an entirely explicit fashion; by analogy it becomes a tacit version of the same thing, which one can either adhere to or not. 'Rule' in its ordinary sense is something both public and explicit. In its analogical sense it is something that is common – that is to say, the same thing can be 'grasped', on the analogy of a physical thing held in the hands, by various people simultaneously, but which is tacit or in some way not reducible to explicit formulation.

These analogical things are not, however, located in a collective mind. They are, rather, meant to be understood as quasi-objects with a certain kind of substance or causal reality of their own. 'Substance' is a source of its own embarrassments. But it solves a basic problem: if the quasi-object is public, and if the same object is accessible to various people, there is no problem about the identity or sameness of the quasi-object that is mutually possessed. This 'solution' proceeds wholly on the level of analogy, of course. But if one can make good on the analogy by solving the problem of how the public thing – rule, convention, ideology or shared tacit knowledge – becomes incorporated in a person, one need not solve the problem of whether the thing incorporated is the *same*. The thing that is 'inside' the individual, in the form of a habit or habit of mind, is the same because the same public quasi-object is being incorporated by different people. This avoids the problem that bedevils the 'private' solution – locating practice in habit alone raises the possibility that genotypes differ. But it does not solve the problem of transmission. The rules or conventions still have to get into the persons who are supposed to share them. There must be a means for transmitting tacit conventions, rules, ideologies and the like.

One strategy for avoiding the choice between habits and collective quasi-objects located in some mysterious social substrate is to use public *objects*, such as texts, as the locus of what is 'shared'. This avoids the problem of location. What is 'shared' is something more mundane, an actual text or a public linguistic pattern. But these arguments trade the location mystery for a worse one. They work only by attributing mysterious causal powers and mechanisms, such as 'hegemonic powers', to texts, overt linguistic patterns and the like. A typical example is this. Mark Poster writes that 'sexual practices are in a good part produced through articulated forms of language'.[17] What this presumably means is that some common or shared forms of overt sexual behaviour are caused – 'produced', as Poster says – by linguistic usages, so that by succumbing to the linguistic usages one is necessarily influenced, partly if not decisively, in one's sexual conduct. 'Articulated forms of language' do not, presumably, *directly* produce sexual activity, but are presumably part of the causal background to the patterns of sexual behaviour that language-users persist in. It is difficult to see how an account of the persistence of the effects of language beyond the moment of reading or speaking could be devised that would not involve 'mental traces' of the kind that in Chapter 2 was said to be the minimal core of the concept of habit. So at best language forms produce habits relevant to sexual conduct.

The private solution: habit

Habit, then, seems to be an ineradicable element of the notion of practice. At some stage in the causal path from practice or text to individual act or performance there is something individual and mental that persists – unlike an impulse passing through the brain. Everyone agrees, it seems, that *something* is carried by habit. Even the most extreme textualists, such as Poster, would not suppose that the influence of texts depends on the actual physical presence of a text, or that its mental presence has to be in the form of conscious memory. But habit does not present itself as a very promising solution to the problem of location, despite its prominence in the history of philosophy and for that matter nineteenth-century social theory.[18] The reason for this is simple. The problem of explaining agreement and disagreement – one of the problems that the other concepts (rule, convention and the collective consciousness) were designed to solve – is not solved by habit. Habits, taken by themselves, are private things. My habits ordinarily differ from yours. There is nothing in habits themselves that assures agreement or makes it possible.

Of course, this does not mean that habits may not be induced in a person in such a way that consistency in public performances, in 'external' behaviour, can be assured. 'Discipline' is the means by which consistency in public performance is assured, as much as possible or needed, for particular purposes. In some people 'training' will not take. But the consistency or 'sameness' in the case of discipline is external. Tacit conventions, rules, collective representations or practices and the like are, in contrast, the same *internally* as well as in their external manifestations. And this sameness is crucial to their main explanatory use. They explain external agreement or sameness between different people by reference to internal facts which are themselves the same between different people, such as *shared* practices, or rules possessed *in common*.

If a practice is indeed 'shared', it is the same practice for each. If an external performance – such as marching on command or doing sums – is habitualized, the habits aren't *necessarily* the same: only the externals need be. This is a point of some importance. If we begin with such mundane performances as riding a bicycle, we can see what is at issue here. Two people may learn to ride a bicycle equally well, in the sense that they are able to perform the same tricks on the bicycle, or guide the bicycle through the same manoeuvres. But each person, in acquiring this skill, has done so with a different instrument, their own body, which they have trained in a different way. The 'differences' may be seen from the history of their teaching themselves the skill or learning it. One person may have taken more time learning one aspect of the performance than another person did, or mastered different elements of the performance in different sequences. So the internal structure of the causal links created by habituation may not be identical. Like Quine's bushes, they are different inside but have been trimmed to be identical in outward appearance.

Not only *may* they not be identical, there is every reason to suppose that they are not identical. A seriously injured person whose body changes as a result of the injury typically needs to relearn a skill, such as the ability to walk or speak. The skill that sufficed for his or her previous body (or brain, in the case of brain injuries) is not sufficient for the production of the same *external* performance with his or her changed body. By the same token, one would suppose that if his or her skill could be transplanted to the body of another person, he or she would have the same kind of difficulty with the production of externally similar performances – he or she would need to relearn, or adapt, the habits acquired to fit with his or her new body. The ability to relearn presumably is to be explained by some sort of causal or feedback process in which habits are regularized or in which they are produced within the individual in such a way that he or she can meet the tests of performance for the skill, so that he or she is able to walk or ride a bicycle.

Sameness of habits, then, is sameness of habitual performance, or perhaps the disposition to produce the same performance under the same conditions, not sameness of the causal history of the acquisition of the habit or sameness of the actual mechanisms by which the habitual action is produced – in relearning a skill one presumably replaces the causal structure that previously produced the performance. The habits persisted after the injury, but could not produce the performance after the injury. After relearning, a new but different internal causal structure of habituation produces the same external performance.

One might claim that this kind of reasoning holds only for *embodied* habits or skills, and argue that *language* is exempt from this kind of consideration because there is no different 'instrument' for the language-user to master. To establish this exemption would require one to show that the habits underlying the use of a given language have some sort of identity absent from embodied skills – that underlying linguistic habits as well as external linguistic performances are 'the same'. And the evidence for their being the same must be other than sameness of external performance. It would be necessary to exclude the possibility that the actual agreement in performance one finds in the use of language can be explained by linguistic habits which differ in different people – have different internal properties or architecture – but produce the same external performances.

For habits, then, sameness of external performance is not necessarily a result of sameness of *internal* structure. So mutuality, agreement or sameness in external performance must be explained differently. As we have seen, this can be done by choosing one of the other locational options – by appealing to the notion of a shared quasi-object, such as a rule in the sense of a tacit rule which is grasped in the same way or internalized by different persons, or by appealing to some sort of dualistic force, such as Tönnies' collective intentions, which come to be habitualized (or acquire the *force* of habit in the individual through repetition). But there is an alternative. The sameness in external performance that needs to be explained can be explained directly. The same kind of causal mechanisms of feedback and correction that figure in the case of relearning skills, for example, may be given as means of accounting for external sameness. This would avoid appeal to the concept of practice altogether. But it would also undermine the notion of a language, a culture, a tradition, a scientific paradigm and the like. These too are shared quasi-objects with an explanatory role analogous to that of practice. And they are much more deeply entrenched in usage.

Location and transmission

The results of the argument so far may be briefly summarized. The basic concepts of practice discussed in earlier chapters were analogical concepts developed for particular explanatory purposes. These purposes included the explanation of understanding, agreement, similarity in behaviour – or their absence. In some cases, the explanatory things, 'presuppositions', 'conventions', 'ideologies', 'rules' and the like, were understood as tacit forms or analogues to things that were not always tacit. This analogical use of these terms had a problem. A convention in the literal 'public' sense has a location, for example in a written document, such as a treaty, which 'contains' the convention. The legal force of a convention of this sort depends on the law; the actual influence of the convention on action depends, initially at least, on the intentions of the signatories. 'Conventions' in the tacit sense have no literal location, and cannot be said to be the subject of intentions of agents, except perhaps in an extended, analogical sense of tacit intentions, because they are tacit. In the same way, they cannot be said to be acquired in the way that a convention ordinarily would be. One can read a treaty. One cannot read what is not written.

Yet to do the explanatory work that these analogical concepts are designed to do – in particular to explain agreement and its absence – it must be at least possible to account for the fact of possession or the absence of possession: for the fact that someone does or does not possess a convention. To be unable to do so means agreement is still a mystery. But the various concepts of practice that we have examined are peculiarly ill suited to this step. To explain how they get to the places they must get to – namely, inside some people and not others – in order to do their explanatory job seems to require an unusual process of transmission. If we conceive of practices as public quasi-objects, they must get from their public location into the persons who act in accordance with them. If we conceive of them as dualistic objects or forces, with collective and individual aspects, we are faced with the problem of how they can interact causally both on the collective and individual level. If we conceive of practices as nothing more than habits, we are faced with the question of how the *same* habits get into different people.

Some of these problems are more easily solved than others. We have already noticed in Chapter 2 the existence of two methods of transmission, imitation and habitualization. Habitualization accounts for the transformation of public things into habits. Public conventions, such as driving on the right-hand side of the road, in time, become habitualized and adherence to these conventions becomes, so to speak, subintentional. Similarly for 'ideology'. An explicit ideology, such as the Calvinist doctrines of salvation examined by Weber in his *The Protestant Ethic and the Spirit of Capitalism*, may, in a given context, define certain attitudes or emotions as sinful, and believers in this ideology may discipline themselves to feel in accordance with the ideology. The attitudes may then become habitual, and no longer require conscious reference to the public expressions of the religious doctrines of Calvinism.

It is a useful historical tactic to identify the explicit formulations of supposed conventions before they become tacit. Weber does this by analysing Calvin's texts – much of his description of the beliefs of his subjects, indeed, is taken directly from Calvin's *Institutes* and attributed to later believers. But this tactic does not solve the problem of the continued transmission of these beliefs once they have become tacit. Weber evades this question by appealing to the notion of ideal-types and suggesting that one can attribute unconscious beliefs and intentions by comparing the actual conduct of people to the conscious, fully intentional case. This is dubious enough as a methodological device – similar manifestations might be the results of different causes. But it fails completely to make sense of transmission: an explicit ideology or convention that has been 'habitualized' was originally transmitted in a familiar way, through reading or hearing. How is a tacit ideology transmitted? Weber's best answer to this is 'imitation'. But only external conduct can be imitated. An inner thing, such as an idea or disposition, cannot be imitated, at least not directly.

This brings us to a fundamental problem. The mechanisms of habitualization and imitation are not a very good model for the processes of transmission that are required by the concept of practice, for reasons that have to do with the problem of location and the problem of sameness. In the standard or basic case of habitualization we begin with something that is literally the same – for example the same treaty is signed by the parties, the same words heard from the pulpit, or the same theological text is read. But the moment the words of the text leave the page, or the sound leaves the mouth of the pastor, or the treaty is read, this sameness ceases. Treaties are subject to interpretation, as are texts and utterances. To be sure one may argue that the reading of texts, interpretation of treaties and hearing of sermons are subject to tacit conventions which assure sameness in the reception of the message that is encoded in the text, treaty or sermon. One may even conclude that the fact that texts and utterances may be interpreted differently shows the necessity of shared tacit interpretive conventions: without such conventions, it may be argued, everyone would, or could, hear the same sounds to mean different things.[19]

But one is faced, in the case of shared tacit conventions, with the problem of sameness all over again. What mechanism of transmission assures that the interpretive conventions are in fact shared – that the conventions I interpret in terms of are the same as the conventions you interpret in terms of? Again, the idea that conventions are shared requires some means of transmitting them that assures that they are the same – that they are, in Bourdieu's phrase, 'reproduced'. Making external behaviour 'the same' through discipline or training is something we understand. But education and discipline both act directly only on performance, *external* behaviour. Making the internal facts of the possession of a convention or presupposition the same is a different matter.

Foucault's 'archeological' studies rely heavily on the historiographical technique employed by Weber, but with a twist. Like Weber, Foucault identifies a text or document that is an early articulation of a doctrine, set of distinctions or justification of a technique, and, like Weber, reasons that this text or document gives in explicit form assumptions or purposes that are subsequently obscured but remain as causal forces. But for Foucault the assumptions are built into the technique or practice and are, so to speak, carried along with the practice by its users, who are themselves transformed or constituted by these techniques into persons with the purposes and dispositions that are borne by the technique. This is the kind of causal influence Poster has in mind when he says that articulated forms of language 'produce' sexual practices – people and their mental habits, on this model, are more plastic than texts or the forms articulated in texts. Texts, of course, are not only more fixed than dispositions, they are unproblematically 'public'.

The model of transmission of practices through texts supposes that there is a kind of transmission that proceeds on the back of the explicit message.[20] The message is a carrier of something else – such as dispositions and preferences. They arrive like the rats on a cargo ship, and get off along with the cargo – inexplicitly or tacitly rather than as part of the message. But as long as we think of these arrivals as things that are reproduced identically inside a person, we face the same problem: the language is purely metaphorical. To make something more of it would require the identification of some sort of process of transmission that assured that the things transmitted were in fact the same. But the same considerations arise in this case as for the direct transmission of practices from one person to another through imitation. 'Imitation' can transmit only by way of externals – what is imitated has to be observed before it is imitated. Some sort of substitute for this process, by which the internal thing, such as the disposition, can be transmitted, needs to be found.

So where does this leave us? If the process of the transmission of practices on the back of ordinary messages is to be taken as a real process for which the evidence is unfortunately limited and indirect, we are faced with the usual problems of examining weak empirical hypotheses. We may examine the evidence and find it to be subject to alternative construals that better fit with the evidence and with what is known causally about mental processes, communication and the like. Here we face the following problem. The processes in question are supposed by the theory to be ubiquitous and pervasive. So we cannot settle for a mechanism that works only in rare circumstances – the mechanism must itself be ubiquitous and pervasive. Yet the mechanism must work in a way that carries the practices to the right people and only to the right people. However it works, the process must be restrictive. It must transmit the practices to the people who possess them, and fail to transmit them to the people who do not possess them.

Sameness 1: 'special moments' solutions

There are several ways to answer this problem, but ordinarily the answers have not taken the form of identifying a mechanism for identical reproduction but have instead tried to identify a special moment in which there is a privileged kind of transmission, or to specify the special circumstances in which the right kind of transmission can occur. The best-established of these traditions is the one which Derrida became celebrated for attacking – the privilege which Plato accorded speech over writing, or more generally the idea that face-to-face interaction or dialogue is a uniquely powerful mode for the conveyance of tacit knowledge.[21] Polanyi and Shils, for example, stress the significance of apprenticeships in intellectual work. As Shils quotes Polanyi, 'Science is an Apostolic Succession'. The mystery of the ceremony of laying on of hands is repeated in the circumstance of joint work in a scientific laboratory. The same idea appears in literary theory. Iser uses sociological terminology invented by Georg Simmel to describe the face-to-face situation as one in which 'the partners in dyadic interaction can ask each other questions in order to ascertain how far their views have controlled contingency, or their images have bridged the gap of inexperienceability of one another's experience'. This situation is explicitly contrasted to the reading of fiction. One cannot ask questions of the participants in the dyadic interactions presented in novels.[22]

Another approach to the problem is to identify a special stage in development in which 'imitation' occurs as a process which is automatic, unreflective, and therefore duplicative. Nietzsche thought that children absorbed morality in this way, and that primitive peoples, conceived in the fashion of the time as childlike, had a moral life composed of imitation and the fear of deviation from the patterns of the human herd. In twentieth-century behavioural science this terminology was replaced by 'socialization', a term that was ultimately applied to such cases as acquiring the proper dispositions and attitudes for the practice of a particular calling, 'professional socialization'. In each of these cases the image remained the same – a moment of plasticity during which 'norms' or other public quasi-objects were 'internalized' or 'introjected'.

Durkheim, following Gustave Le Bon's *The Crowd*, identified yet another kind of moment, in which the individual in immediate contact with a crowd or in the presence of some sort of public social ritual is especially subject to the influence of the collective consciousness.[23] In these moments the internalized demands of morality are revivified, and new moral commands may be erected within the collective consciousness. In some of these moments of collective plasticity there is an effect, which Durkheim describes as collective effervescence, in which the collective consciousness itself becomes plastic and in which novel collective representations and commands simultaneously emerge and become established in the collective consciousness.

These conceptions of the special conditions for acquiring shared quasi-objects such as 'norms' do not directly solve the problem of sameness – the problem of assuring that the internalized thing is a faithful 'reproduction' of the thing that others have internalized. But they do deal indirectly with this problem. The privileged moments are those in which particular sources of individualizing interpretation are eliminated or corrected for. In the case of children or primitives, the idea is that to misinterpret or vary the norms or rules that are available for imitation requires individual intellectual or moral powers that children do not have. Adults may have the intellectual resources to interpret differently and feign conformity, or the moral resources to resist conformity. Children and primitives are subject to large fears and thus are ill equipped to do other than conform, and consequently are plastic and absorb or internalize without 'noise' or disturbances. In the case of face-to-face interaction, the thought is that dialogue enables interpretations to be corrected, or, in the case of laboratory skills, provides for 'coaching' so that the embodied elements of practice, the physical skills, can be passed on along with the intellectual skills which together comprise the tacit knowledge necessary for the work of scientific discovery. The Durkheimian case is one in which the individualizing intellectual and personal impediments to the absorption of collective representations and practices are removed, and in which, to state the point in the locutions of others, reception is pure and reproduction faithful.

The model here is simple – faithful reproduction may be inhibited or blocked by various obstacles, or sources of 'noise'. Remove these, and transmission is perfect. The flaws in this reasoning are, however, serious. The idea of perfect transmission of identical objects is suggested by the idea that there are obstacles to transmission. But even if one removed all the 'obstacles' or 'noise', the copy on the receiving end might differ from that on the sending end – there may be no determinate relation between sending and receiving, no uniquely correct 'reception'. In any case the means of sending, through external manifestations of various kinds, vary considerably, even in the favoured cases. The laboratory experiences of two apprentice scientists are, for example, likely to be quite different. So whatever sameness there is in the tacit knowledge they acquire from the master scientist, it is not going to be the product of being sent the same messages, of having the same experiences or being subject to the same causes unless we are to suppose that the causal processes are occult and not composed of ordinary experiences which differ.

The 'same transmission, same acquisition' model is in any case insufficient to account for the sameness of practices between persons with different experiences. Part of the concept of practice is the idea that *practising* is in some sense a means of acquisition, and that the *same* thing can, at least in the case of some practices, such as the ability to speak a foreign language, be acquired in a different way. This was the case with the example from Berkeley with which we began in Chapter 1. If the concept of practice requires that the 'same' practice can be acquired by different means, there is no point in searching for exact correspondences between transmissions and acquisitions. The rules of a language given in textbooks are themselves 'transmissions'. So even if the same causal conditions or tacit messages produced the same internalized practice, which is itself questionable, the same result may be produced in different ways. This is by no means an unusual situation. One can learn how to utilize a complex computer program, such as a word-processing program, by various means as well. One can memorize the manual and through repeated application habitualize the rules one has memorized. Or one can go through a prescribed series of exercises which are designed to make certain things habitual – to inscribe them on the body, so to speak. Or one can consciously choose to ignore the manual and the prescribed exercises, proceed by trial and error and consciously memorize as little as possible, so as to acquire the habits needed to operate the program unconsciously. The same performances might be produced by persons who learned to run the program in these different ways.

Sameness of practices between persons, then, at least in the externally observable sense, is something distinct from the facts of transmission. Sameness of transmission – obstacle-free, perfect transmission – might conceivably assure sameness of acquisition. But sameness of practices between persons can occur *without* similar transmissions. More generally, the causal history of acquisition is irrelevant to *identity* of practices between persons. So the idea that sameness of practice is assured by sameness of transmission is insufficient, even if true. It can account only for a small subset of the relevant cases.

If there is a variety of means of transmission of the same practice, a set of means for acquisition of the same practice, we have an apparent path to a solution of the problem identified above. If the processes of acquisition must be ubiquitous and pervasive, the mechanism must be ubiquitous and pervasive, but also selective, transmitting to the people who are supposed to possess the practice and not to others. If we conclude that there are a variety of mechanisms, the problem is on its way to being solved – a set of mechanisms, including imitation and the like, may suffice to account for the distribution of practices between persons.

But if there are problems with the notion of transparent, duplicative transmission itself, this approach will not solve it. Rather this approach substitutes a variety of new explanatory problems – first, the problem of explaining separately, for each of these different forms of transmission, how duplicative transmission is possible; and second, the problem of explaining how it is possible for these different forms of transmission, each with its own kind of noise or error and each dependent on the special capacities of reception of the persons transmitted to, to produce the *same* practice in the different people who receive these transmissions. The multi-method solution to the problem of transmission, in short, produces its own problem of mutuality, analogous to the problem that arose in connection with the 'habit' model of practices. If practices travel from person to person, or from texts to persons, or from the collective ether to persons in different ways, how do they produce the same effects – the internalization of the same practices – in each person?

One can, of course, imagine 'solutions' to this problem or, more precisely, invent more analogies to solve them. One might say, for example, that the messages received from different sources are somehow sorted by an internal sifter so that the common denominator comes out. But the hard core of the problem is that it would be a miracle, on the order of the miraculous agreement between the seventy separate translations of the Bible known as the Septuagint, for the tacit messages received to be the same. Everything we know about the way in which, for example, face-to-face interactions work suggests otherwise. The message Xenophon received from Socrates, at least on the evidence of Xenophon's writings, was very different from the message Plato received. Was this simply a sign of lack of capacity to receive on the part of Xenophon?[24] And if so, if people are graded by their capacities to receive, is there any reason to suppose that messages passed to and from a large number of such people would be anything more than a jumble?

So we arrive at a situation in which the mildly exotic hypothesis with which we began, the notion of a common possession of a tacit object, must be preserved by increasingly fantastic auxiliary hypotheses. It begins to appear that the idea of the common possession of a tacit quasi-object – a shared practice – is a myth in the Lévi-Straussian sense, a way of solving the problem of the binary opposition between privacy and public agreement, which generates its own mythic conflict over transmission, which needs another mythic solution.

Sameness 2: the case of rules

There is a simple way out of the problem of multiple messages carried through multiple and imperfect carriers. If one imagines an object-like,

68 *Transmission*

commonly possessed thing that the messages can be referred back to or checked against, that is to say, something that is not dependent on imperfect transmission and on these transmissions magically agreeing, the model of 'shared practices' may be saved. We may begin a consideration of this solution with what might be regarded as the strongest case of sameness of practices, the tacit rules underlying the practices of elementary mathematics. Saul Kripke's discussion of Wittgenstein's account of the impossibility of a private language is a convenient starting point. Kripke, unlike Wittgenstein, gives what may be taken as a general account of rules that itself amounts to a kind of social theory – what has been called 'the rules model of culture'.[25]

Wittgenstein's own uses of these concepts are part of a specific sort of therapeutic resolution of philosophical problems which does not depend on the same kinds of commitments – the whole vocabulary of 'rules', 'language games' and the like that Wittgenstein employs may be seen as a ladder of the sort one kicks away after climbing. But there is a social theoretical moment in Wittgenstein as well, one which parallels the moment at which Hume appeals to custom. It occurs in the text quoted in Chapter 1, in which Wittgenstein speaks of the 'inherited background', and in his much-disputed appeal to the concept of *Lebensformen*, 'forms of life'. The term was a technical usage of the pedagogical philosopher and sociologist Eduard Spranger.[26]

Spranger's aim in his book *Lebensformen* is to understand understanding in terms of the background to understanding. Different types of people have different experiences in the world, each of which is limited. In particular, there is a limit to philosophical understanding or theoretical abstraction, to the power of the 'theoretical attitude' to comprehend. Our understanding of other persons cannot consist wholly in understanding their 'linguistic expressions' and 'physical signs'. 'Further acts of understanding' that 'lie behind' them are necessary:

> I can understand what someone says but beyond that is raised the question: (1) do I understand the speaker or writer, of whom the report is only an infinitesimal section as a total being? It may be that he makes a mistake or that he wants to lie, that he lives under special conditions which I fail to understand, or that he is my intellectual superior to such an extent that I am incapable of understanding him. Christ's words: 'Blessed are they that hunger and thirst after righteousness for they shall be filled' are comprehensible to me since I speak the language. But do I understand him? – And (2) do I really understand the whole significance of these words? Certainly I understand them as words which have been combined

to form a grammatical sentence. But it is quite a different matter whether or not I understand their religio-ethical meaning. In both cases the physical objectivation of the mental factor into words is only a preliminary aid.[27]

Spranger uses the term 'preunderstanding' to denote the background to understanding. If a 'preunderstanding' is a hidden tacit object, the same questions (What sort of object is it? How does it get transmitted?) need to be asked. But Spranger's point is different. Although Spranger insists 'that society is an overindividual context of effects' that 'determines from the beginning every individual's whole mental structure', and he sees this context as the result of historical development, his point is that every individual's experience of this context is only partial. This holds for the sociologist too: 'The complexly interwoven inner structure of sociological formations is forever beyond our cognition and understanding'.[28] The best that sociologists can do is to typify – hence his own attempt to distinguish particular typical partial attitudes, such as the economic, theoretical, religious, aesthetic, social and political.[29] These types are themselves only fictions, never found in pure form in reality.[30] So for Spranger the individual's experience of the historico-cultural background that is shared with others is distinctive. There is no internalized common object. The preunderstandings that enable one to understand Christ's saying are effects of the social, historical, cultural context, but not, so to speak, standardized effects that are the same for all.

The inherited background of which Wittgenstein wrote is open to a similar interpretation: a background is a common thing, which Spranger thinks of as an objective mind (and therefore possessing a 'structure') but a thing experienced differently by different people, with different effects, enabling them to understand different things. Two points need to be made about this account. One is that it is not 'the rules model of culture', because the historico-mental world which is the cultural context is not composed of rules.[31] The other is that our acquisition of culture differentiates or individualizes us. If we read Kripke's account of Wittgenstein, we get a quite different picture. Kripke presents Wittgenstein as the author of a particular account of rules or practices. Kripke's model of the acquisition of rules is extremely simple: one either 'gets it' or one doesn't.

Kripke argues that Wittgenstein's achievement in the private-language argument was to invent a new kind of scepticism over whether one is in fact following the same rules as other persons, a problem at the heart of the general problem of sameness discussed here. Kripke's formulation has the potential of altering the problem decisively, by redefining the problem of 'sameness' itself. He considers two rules, addition and quaddition, both of which might be taken to be the meaning of the term 'plus'. His argument proceeds by analysing the assertability conditions for assertions about what rules someone is following. The statement 'Jones means addition [rather than quaddition or something else] by "plus"' may be asserted by Jones himself on certain grounds, and by other observers, such as Smith, on certain different grounds.

> *Jones* is entitled, subject to correction by others, provisionally to say 'I mean addition by "plus,"' whenever he has the feeling of confidence – 'now I can go on!' – that he can give 'correct' responses in new cases; and he is entitled, again provisionally, and subject to correction by others, to judge a new response to be 'correct' simply because it is the response he is inclined to give. These inclinations (both Jones' general inclination that he has 'got it' and his particular inclination to give particular answers in particular addition problems) are to be regarded as primitive. They are not to be justified in terms of Jones' ability to interpret his own intentions or anything else.[32]

It is not, however, for the individual to judge whether he has 'got it'. The 'community' makes this determination:

> Smith need *not* accept Jones' authority on these matters: Smith will judge Jones to mean addition by 'plus' only if he judges that Jones' answers to particular addition problems agree with those *he* is inclined to give, or, if they occasionally disagree, he can interpret Jones as at least following the proper procedure.... If Jones consistently fails to give responses in agreement (in this broad sense) with Smith's, Smith will judge that he does not mean addition by 'plus'. Even if Jones did mean it in the past, the present deviation will justify Smith in judging that he has lapsed.[33]

'In point of fact', Kripke claims, stating what he takes to be Wittgenstein's case, 'our actual community is (roughly) uniform in its practices with respect to addition'. So Smith's judgments, taken together with the judgments of others, are a kind of test – and ultimately the sole test – of Jones' claim to have mastered the concept of addition:[34]

An individual who passes such tests is admitted into the community as an adder; an individual who passes such tests in enough other cases is admitted as a normal speaker of the language and a member of the community.[35]

And this is all there is to possessing a concept.

When we ... attribute concepts to individuals, we depict no special 'state' of their minds [but] we do something of importance. We take them provisionally into the community, as long as further deviant behaviour does not exclude them. In practice, such deviant behaviour rarely occurs.[36]

This appeal to the concept of 'community and community membership is not intended to give 'community' some special sort of ontological status or causal power – to make it into some sort of substrate *à la* Durkheim or cause of correct inclination in the manner of Tönnies. As Kripke interprets Wittgenstein, the concept of 'form of life' underlies the notion of community, rather than the reverse. 'The entire "game" we have described – that the community attributes a concept to an individual so long as he exhibits sufficient conformity, under test circumstances, to the behaviour of the community – would lose its point outside a community that generally agrees in its practices'.[37] A 'form of life' is 'the set of responses in which we agree, and the way they interweave with our activities'.[38] So the fact that is fundamental is the existence of agreement.

Among the implications of this general line of reasoning are the following. It is intelligible to doubt whether one is in fact following the same rule as one was previously following – this is Wittgenstein's 'new form of scepticism'. But more important, for our purposes, is that the traditional notion of possession of concepts is wrong:

On Wittgenstein's conception, a certain type of traditional – and overwhelmingly natural – explanation of our shared form of life is excluded. We cannot say that we all respond as we do to '68 + 57' *because* we all grasp the concept of addition in the same way, that we share common responses to particular addition problems *because* we have a common concept of addition. . . . For Wittgenstein, an explanation of this kind ignores his [novel form of scepticism]. . . . There is no objective fact –

that we all mean addition by '+', or even that a given individual does – that explains our agreement in particular cases. Rather our license to say of each other that we mean addition by '+' is part of a 'language game' that sustains itself only because of the brute fact that we generally agree (nothing about 'grasping concepts' guarantees that it will not break down tomorrow).[39]

The 'brute fact' of agreement, in short, is all the fact there is to a rule. Rules are not found in some sort of collective ether, or in the substrate of the social; nor are the inclinations rule-following requires themselves 'social' or collective. There is also no 'objective' fact of the matter.

Wittgenstein's concept of a rule seems at first blush to be simply another metaphorical use of a concept with a particular more or less clear meaning when used to refer to the explicit case and a much more mysterious meaning when used to refer to the tacit case. In the explicit case a rule is an object that is intentional: people have to think of it as a rule, and if it is thought of in the right way it is a rule. In the tacit case there is no 'thinking of' – there is only 'acting as if'. The only criteria for following a rule must be external. The tests that must be passed to establish possession must be external as well – tests applied, in the last instance, by members of the same community. But Kripke's account is nevertheless a radical departure from the idea of rule as a mysterious quasi-object with causal powers that explain agreement.

The existence of a shared rule does not explain the mutuality or agreement that holds between the users of elementary mathematics. It is rather the reverse – agreement is the primitive fact. Mutuality is possible *because of* the fact of agreement. Agreement is the prior fact, the condition. One can enforce tests of agreement or play the language game of attribution of meaning because there is agreement. When agreement ceases, the game can no longer be played. 'Getting it', in the case of a rule, is not getting a message which must then be decoded or internalized: acquisition is simply achieving agreement. There is no separate fact of transmission, which leads to agreement, and which is then validated by tests – rather, the tests serve only as a check on whether agreement has been achieved.

But the radicalism of the departure is only apparent. 'Agreement' is itself used here in a special, metaphorical sense, to mean something tacit and sub-intentional. In other cases, as we have seen, these extended usages have proven troublesome because of their ontological implications – typically they generated quasi-objects that had to be conceived in peculiar ways, especially in relation to transmission. As I have suggested, in some cases, such as Durkheim and Tönnies, the ontology itself, built up from analogies to causal mechanisms from nineteenth-century science, became – at least to present ears – fantastic. In other cases, the troubles showed up with the notion of transmitting the same things – reproducing them inside another person. The problem was that the mechanisms themselves did not assure the sameness of the internalized thing – there were no 'sameness-preserving' modes of transmission and acquisition, whether the transmissions were mediated by public quasi-objects, such as conventions, or by actual public objects, such as texts, which are of course open to interpretation.

Does Kripke's conception of a Wittgensteinian rule, by collapsing transmission into agreement, avoid these problems? And if so, is it a solution to the problem of practice generally? The two questions are closely connected. Elementary mathematics forms for Kripke's Wittgenstein a paradigm for the process of rule acquisition and for rule-following. The problem, however, is broader. Does this process correspond to all the relevant cases – to Mauss' 'American walk' as well as Spranger's Christian message? Wittgenstein himself seems to have thought of forms of life as Spranger did, as the *background* to belief, communication, and to rules themselves. Kripke's Wittgenstein, in contrast, has only brute agreements. The background of which Wittgenstein speaks seems to be a background composed of something shared and specific to a particular group of people – something *inherited* – which is *unlike* rules in the sense of the rules of elementary mathematics. For Kripke, only rules are inherited. The only kind of transmission he envisions is the transmission of rules, and the only kind of cultural stuff he conceives is rules.

Familiar difficulties arise immediately on extending the model beyond mathematics. Many of the terms in a language do not have the kind of clear criteria of application assumed by the model – the rules governing them are, as the phrase goes, open-textured. Admitting that usage does not correspond mechanically to ideal models is, indeed, essential to salvaging the explanatory uses of the notion of rules. Unless rules permit a certain openness of application, it becomes impossible to explain how usages shift in response to novel situations and in novel applications. Novel applications would, indeed, be ruled out by the Kripkean model strictly applied. Where the rule was not a matter of agreement, in Kripke's terms, there is no rule at all.

A serious difficulty with the case of open-textured rules arises over transmission and acquisition. If a rule may be somewhat vague, what precisely is being passed on? Is it the *same* rule along with all its ambiguities and openness? What of shifts in usage through extension to novel applications? Is a novel agreement among all members of the community of users reached on each occasion of its extended application? (Alternatively, is the community of users defined by agreement with the extended usage?) Or is it rather that there is nothing in the way of a rule that is *precisely the same* between people – that some people are inclined to use and understand words in ways that are subtly (and sometimes not so subtly) different from other people?

Kripke's account would say that rules are rules, and are transmitted in the same fashion whether they are open-textured or not. They are passed on in the same way because in each case possessing a rule is achieving and continuing agreement. The rule on which agreement occurs is the 'same' rule for each person, by definition. But this is wildly implausible. The natural interpretation is that people come to understand the same thing in different ways, based on their experiences with the words and the feedback they receive from their use and from understanding them in particular ways. Much of this feedback may be consistent with a given understanding, and their understanding may be close enough to those of other persons for them to get by tolerably. But their understanding, meaning the places that they would apply the terms or claim to understand their use, would vary slightly if not greatly. The community of language-users is one in which there are many slightly 'deviant' persons, and perhaps even a good number of fairly seriously deviant ones and perhaps no perfect speakers. Kripke, however, must reason differently – he must say that the 'agreement' that is the brute fact at the basis of a rule must be a univocal thing, the same for everyone who is a party to it. Even if it is vague or open-textured, it must be vague and open-textured in the *same way* for all parties in the community constituted by the agreement.

The strangeness of this reasoning becomes apparent as soon as one considers the 'brute fact' of agreement, which turns out to be not so brutish at all. 'Agreement' turns out, on reflection, to mean different things in different contexts. In particular practical settings the purposes at hand may be served by what we may sense, in contrast to other situations involving the same concepts, to be a very modest agreement or mutuality. In others, the problems of understanding what other persons want and mean are endemic, seemingly insoluble, and perhaps beyond our capacity. Unbridgeable gaps of experienceability, as Iser would put it, prevent our getting a sense of sharing that we consider adequate for the purposes. In the cases of religion and love, there may be a want of mutuality or agreement that is always felt more or less strongly and overcome only mystically. But to speak in this phenomenological way about mutuality goes beyond Kripke's way of looking at the issue. The sense of having 'gotten it', is after all just a sense, and always open to scepticism. We may not have gotten it – or we may have gotten all there is to get and are mistakenly pining for something more.

Kripke's Wittgenstein has a response to this: the community provides us with 'tests' of our having 'gotten' a practice. So the notion of getting it turns out to require the not so brutish fact of tests. And the appeal to community 'tests' turns out, on examination, to have familiar defects. The 'tests' to which Kripke refers are themselves wholly analogical, except in his favoured cases of elementary mathematics. Schoolchildren do take tests to see if they have mastered addition – literal tests, on pieces of paper with numbers written on them. There are no such tests for most of the practices that are transmitted as part of a 'form of life'. There are, of course, good and bad experiences, confusions, misunderstandings that are corrected by talk or new evidence of meaning, and so on – but these are not 'tests'. They allow for all the everyday doubts one has over 'understanding'.[40]

Kripke's Wittgenstein, then, avoids a defective analogical account of the transmission of rules, but only by a kind of sleight of hand. He disposes of the problem of transmission by defining acquisition and agreement as identical, and treating agreement as a primitive concept, a brute fact. But the guarantee of sameness in transmission turns out to rest not on this brute fact – mistakes are possible, if not endemic – but on the powers of the community to test for deviance.[41] The tests become the substitute for the common quasi-objects of the other theories – they have the function in the theory of assuring the preservation of sameness. But, like the common quasi-objects of the other theories, such as shared practices, the tests are *themselves* analogical objects, whose 'sameness' is also analogical. But it is a poor analogy. There is nothing about the 'tests' to which a person's acquisitions of rules are put in ordinary social interaction or speech that assures that the 'same' rules are being followed.

The ability of a person to interact more or less successfully with the 'members of a community' (itself a wholly analogical notion, as though a community was a country club with a membership committee) is a matter of habit, a matter of having successfully responded to feedback and having developed habits of response that enable, among other things, the person's various purposes to be achieved. But nothing in the process of feedback or interaction produces, as far as we can tell, sameness. The case of elementary mathematics, where there are literal

76 Transmission

public tests, is part of the small subset of cases in which habits are consciously disciplined. But the discipline is addressed, necessarily, to external manifestations, to performances, and not to the internal structure of the habits themselves. So external, not internal, uniformity is the observable product of discipline.

Sameness 3: rules, social minds or habits?

Kripke's account begins with a subset of rules, namely rules transmitted by discipline, and treats them as a paradigm case of the possession and transmission of rules. It is attractive as a paradigm case because it salvages sameness. It fails, at least in its extended, analogical uses, because the kind of sameness needed to extend the model, for example to the more problematic cases of open-textured rules, differs from the kind of sameness the theory depends on. Kripke's model depends on tests, tests that establish sameness of external performance. What is needed to preserve the concept of sameness in the case of open-textured rules is some analogous means, some way of distinguishing variation of habits, or the acquisition of a variant rule, from the acquisition of the same open-textured rule. Kripke can only make this distinction analogically, and the analogy is strained. It does not fit with our everyday knowledge of the acquisition of habits.

The options with which this discussion of transmission began included two that depended on some sort of shared thing, and one that did not. The one that did not was what I called the habit model. The considerations that could be brought to bear on the selection of one model over another were, I conceded, weak. We are dealing, after all, with analogies applied to subjects for which our evidence is indirect. But these weak considerations turned out to be too tough for at least two of the options, those that involved the notion of a shared object-like practice.

Transmitting this thing, at least in the same form, required hypothesized mechanisms that did not fit with what we know about causal processes. The various 'magic moment' models, in which perfect transmission was supposed to occur, faced two problems: one that the mechanism of perfect transmission itself was mysterious. The other was that the supposed special moments could not be made to match up to the range of cases for which they needed to account. The analogy with consciously disciplined learning, though tempting, was also defective, for reasons that become clear in connection with Kripke. There are no 'tests' of the sort envisioned.

In all these cases, from Durkheim and Tönnies to Foucault and Poster, sameness is the problem – the thing which cannot be transmitted by the means they countenance. The means can be reconceived or supplemented to solve this problem. But the supplements involve increasingly fantastic analogies and auxiliary hypotheses. We are left, then, with the only apparent alternative – the ugly-duckling concept of habit. If the idea of preserving sameness is removed from the other cases of transmission, they collapse into the case of the acquisition of habits, habits which may vary in internal structure and produce performances that are externally the same, and habits which may produce performances that vary slightly but are sufficiently intelligible or sufficiently predictable for the purposes at hand.

The idea of sameness itself may seem like a rhetorical imposition of my own. The writers who appeal to such notions as 'shared practices' ordinarily do not stress that the practices must be 'the same' in order to perform the explanatory tasks to which the concept of practice is assigned. And indeed, the notion of sameness, in such forms as Bourdieu's term 'reproduction' or the Parsonsian notion of the internalization of norms, *is* a case of explanatory overkill. The modest statistical consistencies in attitudes of 'distinction' among French schoolboys obviously do not demand the hypothesis that they share the 'same' practices. Something similar may be said for cases of political culture. Bellah's 'habits of the heart', which are the causal conditions of American individualism, need not be some sort of common quasi-object. Speaking of them as though they are is a kind of fancy talk, a way of making sociological studies of 'attitudes' seem deeper than they are. But if in some cases, the concept is overkill, in other cases it is not. Political traditions, culture and science – the domains of Oakeshott, T.S. Eliot and Polanyi – seem in particular to resist any sort of 'reduction to habit'. These are problems of the 'second-level' uses of the concept of practice, to which I now turn.

5
Change and History

Habits die with individuals. If something persists in history, it cannot be habits alone. Traditions do persist. So traditions cannot consist of habits. This is a simple formulation of a problem with no simple solution. In the past this reasoning has usually been used to support the idea that traditions persist by virtue of some persisting element, such as a force lodged in the collective consciousness, or in *mores* with some sort of inherent power to persist. If it is a fact that patterns of behaviour persist in ways that cannot be accounted for by the influence of causes other than some persisting element, the 'habits' solution described in the last chapter is faced with a serious problem.

These considerations weigh heavily on the side of some notion of a persisting supra-individual element. Indeed, the best that can be said for some of the notions criticized in the last chapter is that they help make sense of persistence, in that they at least point to a cause of the persistence – even if the cause itself is not very plausible. Moreover, the notions of tradition, paradigm, the *longue durée* of the 'structures of everyday life', culture, *habitus*, *Weltanschauung*, and so forth each have a certain hold by virtue of the more or less successful uses to which they have been put. 'Paradigm' makes sense of the mutuality that exists within a given historical community of scientists, and of the distinctness of this community from other communities. Like the concept of practices, concepts such as paradigm, tradition and culture have instrumental value. They help make sense of the beliefs of others and the way these beliefs hang together. So the idea of paradigm or culture is useful as a descriptive concept or as an aid to making sense of the behaviour of others regardless of whether or not one can sustain a simple model of the causal structure of a paradigm as a set of practices imprinted on members of the community or culture. In the case of practices, it appeared that the concept ran into a particular difficulty. It was difficult to construct an account of a practice that fitted with available accounts of the transmission of practices. Practices are supposed to be 'shared', and it should be the case that the same practice can be transmitted to another person. But no account of the process of transmission could explain how the same thing got into different people. Dropping the notion of 'sameness', however, reduced the practices to habits.

If we conceive of culture simply as a body of practices or set of 'rules', we face familiar difficulties about transmission. It is even less plausible to think that a complete set of connected practices, a framework, is transmitted in such a way that it is the same for each member of the society. Yet the standard behavioural science models of culture appeal to such a model. A culture is considered as a kind of package of norms, values, rules and framing devices which is a unified whole and which is transmitted through 'socialization' as a whole. This can be thought of as a simplification or abstraction in the face of complexity, and one might claim that some such simplification is necessary to explain cultural systems, but essentially harmless.

So tradition, culture and similar useful concepts present a series of difficulties that the conclusions of the last chapter, which were after all rather weak, need to accommodate. The instrumental value of the concepts of culture and similar concepts can be readily accommodated, along the lines of the discussion of the psychological reality of 'presuppositions' in Chapter 3. There is nothing about the 'habits' account that is inconsistent with the utility of such hypotheses. The problem is with the distinctive empirical facts that sustain the notions of culture, paradigm and tradition. If these cannot be handled in terms of habituation, we may need to reconsider the notion of a persisting collective fact. We may be able to construct such a notion in a way that avoids the problems with the transmission of practices. These might not be the only options – the problems of persistence may be open to different solutions entirely.

The facts of persistence and inaccessibility

The appeal of the concept of tradition and its variants rests on two main groups of 'facts'. The first is the anomalous persistence of patterns of

80 *Change and History*

behaviour. The second is the difficulty of understanding other cultures. Both groups of facts suggest that there is something like a body of practices that operates behind the puzzling behaviour and accounts for it. With tradition, as with practices generally, we infer the existence of something hidden. The question that arises is the same. Is there an alternative account of the supposed manifestations of the hidden thing?

To answer this question we need first to cast a cold eye on the facts themselves. The crucial 'empirical' fact of the anomalous persistence of traditions, *mores* and the like, for example, is usually understood to be explained by the persistence of the tacit or hidden part. Two aspects of this fact may be distinguished. One is the apparent imperviousness of attitudes, values and the like to governmental action or conscious modification. 'Stateways cannot change folkways', according to the slogan of Sumner, a slogan strikingly supported by the re-emergence of traditional patterns in Eastern European countries after a half-century of suppression under communist rule. The second is that patterns of conduct can be observed to persist in radically different environments and historical settings linked only by the facts of common inheritance. Even quite specific patterns of private conduct, for example, may persist for centuries among persons with a common ethnic or regional genealogy. David Hackett Fischer gives examples of such 'folkways' in his study of the persistence of the local cultures of particular English counties in American communities of emigrants over centuries.[1] These patterns of conduct are not the part of any explicit ideology, and indeed the explicit religious ideologies of the persons who exhibit these patterns of conduct have changed far more radically than the conduct itself. This suggests that there is a secret or hidden pathway by which these patterns are transmitted, and a hidden level which is the substrate in which the patterns inhere. The same sorts of anomalies arise in other contexts, such as the persistence of national scientific styles after emigration.[2] This kind of persistence does not require any hypothesis about transmission, but it does support the idea that there are common cultural 'frames' even in science that scientists carry with them throughout their lives.

This is an elusive bunch of 'facts', however. The major difficulty in dealing with them is conceptual. What sort of identity – sameness – is at stake in claims about the persistence of tradition? One can find startling cases of 'persistence', such as the fact that the daughters of the Chinese communist leader Deng Xiaoping, elderly and unable to speak intelligibly, claimed to understand him and therefore to be his authoritative interpreters, just as in the imperial past daughters of senile and incoherent emperors made the same claims. The reversion to pre-war patterns of political argumentation and bureaucratic intrigue in the post-communist states of Eastern Europe is equally striking. Alan Macfarlane has made claims about the persistence of English individualism from the times of the Germanic tribes described by Tacitus to the present.[3] In each of these cases, it is not clear what sort of sameness is at stake, but it is evident that it is sameness that must be assessed by the historical observer rather than the participants.

'Persistence' is anomalous only for the historian – it is the historian's expectations that are challenged. The things that are noticed as anomalies are precisely the kinds of things that the historian notices out of the mass of historical fact because there *is* a past analogue such as the daughters of dying emperors. Worse, the idea of anomalousness, like other arguments for the existence of non-public collective causal facts on the order of *mores*, depends on the idea that there are no other causal accounts of the same facts – that there is an unexplained causal residue that the concept of *mores* or its analogues explains. This is a very difficult case to make, simply because the burden of proof lies on the maker. One must first exclude coincidence. Then it must be shown that there are no persistent *causes* other than tradition that sustain the fact in its persistence. In the case of Deng's daughters, one might invoke Thomas Wolfe's dictum that people in the same profession tend to be the same the world over, and note that Woodrow Wilson's wife performed the same function at his deathbed, absent any Chinese traditions.

The difficulty of the task of excluding other explanations is compounded by the fact that many cases of persistence can be plausibly accounted for by arguments to the effect that the same thing, such as a ritual, may be caused or causally supported by different things at different times. A coming-of-age ceremony originally sponsored by the East German state, the *Jugendweihe*, for example, has persisted, stripped of its communist trappings, after the dissolution of this state. But this was an invented tradition. Invented traditions with fake historical pedigrees seem often to persist just as well as those with a real past.[4] So the problem of constructing a causal account that eliminates other explanations is likely to be severe. Similar difficulties arise in interpreting the failure of stateways to change folkways. If the 'stateway' was itself based on mistaken causal premises about the thing it wished to change – and this has usually been the case with state interventions into social problems – the lesson of failure is interpretable without recourse to the notion of special persistence.

The second major 'empirical fact' that supports the idea of a tradition is the relative difficulty of comprehending the writings of an intellectual tradition in which one was not trained. The inaccessibility of variant intellectual or cultural traditions goes beyond the difficulty of mastering the 'information' contained in the texts, but is more easily accounted for as a result of failing to possess (or to have properly mastered) the relevant interpretive schemes or tacit assumptions. This has led to the idea that there is a major distinction between two kinds of access to traditions – access through initiation (which is supposed to be superior), and access through other means, such as emulation, translation or mimicry (which are supposed to be inferior). The analogy with language, taken to have similar properties, is typically central to this distinction. MacIntyre, for example, distinguishes between learning an alien philosophical tradition as a 'second first language' and merely translating the vocabulary of one tradition into the vocabulary of the other. He assumes that any such translation will be defective or inadequate because it will embody the assumptions or conceptual usages of the tradition of the metalanguage, the language into which the alien tradition is translated, when what is needed is for this language and body of usages to be enlarged.[5]

The fact of difficulty in understanding is open to various interpretations. One interpretation is that the people who learn something as a first language have indeed come into the possession of some sort of set of common practices that cannot be acquired in any other way. But this interpretation carries with it all the burdens of the notion of practices discussed in the last chapter. There is no evidence that anyone 'shares' in such a common object – no evidence, at least, that cannot be accounted for by the notion of the formation of individual habits that enable people to interact and perform successfully. But the notion of commonly possessed practices has another explanatory use that gives it some attractions that the 'habits' model lacks. If it is the case that we are locked into our 'paradigm' or world-view in such a way that we cannot absorb information or ways of thinking that are contrary to this world-view, we will persist in holding this view. And if our children or students have *de facto* no access to training in any world-view but ours, they will acquire our world-view for want of any alternative. So the inaccessibility of other ways of thinking can be thought of as an account of the persistence of the ways of thinking that make up a given culture.

The attractions of this line of reasoning are considerable. In the first place, it avoids what was a problem for writers like Sumner, who could conceive of the *mores* as powerful and persistent objects, but who could never manage an explanation of why they were so persistent. This reasoning accounts for persistence internally: the features that define the object for us descriptively also serve to explain the fact that they persist. But explaining persistence in this way creates a problem about explaining change – a problem that is in some respects more intractable than the problem of persistence.

Change

The problem with change is difficult to state in any precise way, but the general outlines are simple. If culture is conceived as a set of basic rules that shape experience, including experience of the external world, there is a problem over the question of how these rules change. The term 'basic' is crucial. If one can pick out (or hypothesize the existence of) some set of rules that accounts for patterns of conduct or belief that are highly persistent, one can explain persistence by reference to these rules, and then account for the basic rules themselves in some other manner. The same thing that makes basic rules impervious to change – that they are 'basic' – makes them impervious to explanation. Sumner's notion of *mores* is an instance of this problem. He made the concept fundamental, and emphasized that the *mores* were not subject to alteration by the usual causes that operate on human agents. He had his troubles over the next step, the step of explaining the *mores*, precisely because there was no obvious next step.

The usual next step would be to seek some higher and prior consideration that explained particular different cultural systems as instances. The process of evolution was the consideration favoured by Sumner. Functionalist explanations were favoured by sociologists and anthropologists for much of this century. The idea that there is some sort of external fact or consideration of this kind that accounts for these changes helps preserve the model of 'basic' rules. But it leads to a series of historiographic problems.

The problems are exemplified by Kuhn's notion of paradigm shifts. Paradigms, on one construction, are hidden, tacit premisses that are constitutive of scientific facts and therefore immune to revision on the basis of these facts. What happens, according to Kuhn, is that 'anomalies' – meaning problems that can't be resolved within the system – pile up. At some point a paradigm is abandoned in favour of an alternative paradigm. The neo-Kantian origins of this way of thinking are evident. Weber's version of neo-Kantianism focuses the issues in terms of the concept of 'value'. Values are supposed by him to change between epochs, making the concerns and categories employed in one epoch or another meaningless to those of another epoch. We can perhaps, he thought, reconstruct the categories of past historical epochs, but in the face of them we are like 'a Chinese' facing occidental culture and its categories.

Discontinuity, however, is a dubious phenomenon. Kuhn had trouble making this into a convincing story for science. For culture generally, it is even less plausible, Foucault, motivated by a parallel historiographic problem, strove to divide epochs sharply, as have other historians of culture. But for the most part, the following is true. Small changes, in succession, made the present 'different'. Yet each of these small changes may well have seemed, from the point of view of the participants, to preserve 'sameness' in the sense that was relevant to them. At no point, perhaps, did they have any sense of the 'inaccessibility' of the culture of their parents or teachers. If the past is another country, it did not become so overnight.

Weber was centrally concerned with accounting for changes in cultural preoccupations, and his studies of the effects of religious ideology on practical economic ethics exemplify this concern. But in his methodological essays, the changes in preoccupations and value commitments appear as a mysterious process of succession – the cultural 'light', the light by virtue of which historical problems and objects may be constituted for us as analysts, 'moves on', as he puts it. A fine image – but his own studies of values are *not* accounts of how the light of cultural preoccupations moves on. They are instead causal genealogies, examining the filiations, descent and transformation of *explicitly formulated* ideas as they are habitualized and applied in practice.

This discrepancy is rooted in the kind of object a *Weltanschauung* is and the work it performs for the *analyst*, as against the work it does for the *methodologist*. It, and such analogous objects as *epistemes* and paradigms, are big-block concepts. They aggregate and provide a summary analysis of many small facts about the beliefs and conduct of individuals. Constructing a convincing summary lends the results a certain factual substance. This factual substance comes to have a certain explanatory substance as well, if only by virtue of serving as a convenient middle term or connecting link in an explanation. If 'Victorian sexuality' can be explained by particular patterns of childrearing among the middle classes, it becomes an explanatory fact as well as a summary description. And indeed the summary descriptions, and the explanatory link between 'Victorian sexuality' and the instances of behaviour it subsumes may come to seem far more substantial and compelling than the prior causal link to the supposed explanation of Victorian sexuality.

Such aggregate facts of course lend themselves to big-block explanations, of the sort made famous by Marx in his theory of the *Überbau*, which appealed to the big fact of the succession of epochs of domination by one class or another. The 'ideology' of a class may be teleologically connected to the big-block facts. A class's mode of domination may be aided by the beliefs of the class, or a religious ideology may serve functionally to promote the continued existence of a religious organization. But these explanations are not accounts of causal relations between big-block facts and ideas, but are, typically, accounts of the fate of classes or social groups who are the bearers of the ideas. They deal only with circumstances which help explain the persistence of the bearers of the ideas and the origin of social types. They are not accounts of how novel 'dominant ideologies' arise and how these novel ideas are made intelligible and persuasive to those who adopt them, people who have, presumably, been brought up in a different tradition.[6]

It is appropriate to ask how, given the theory of paradigms, new ideas could be intelligible to the possessors of a given tradition or paradigm. The light of the great cultural concerns that 'moves on' can do so only in this way. Yet the notion of tradition itself seems to rule out any such change. The problem may be seen in terms of the analogy with codes discussed in the last chapter. If the messages we receive are all in code, and if the information we get must pass through and be sorted by our decoding devices (our traditions), or if we can accept only information in a certain code (the language of our tradition), the following question arises: In what code are the decoding devices or their rules transmitted and received? We have two alternatives in the face of this question. The first alternative is this: if the 'rules' themselves are written in the same code as everything else we receive, then this material is, so to speak, simply a form of information. Because it is in the same language, there should be no problem in gaining access to our own code and its rules. The codes and decoding devices of other people would, similarly, be in the language of their tradition. If translation of the 'information' in these traditions was possible, translation of their codes and coding rules would also be possible. We would already have, by hypothesis, access to the language. If this were the case, there would be no particular problem of incommensurability, inadequacy of translation between traditions or paradigms, and so forth. The second is to think that our most basic assumptions and the most basic assumptions of others, understood as their encoding and decoding rules, are in a code that is indecipherable to us through our ordinary decoding rules, which would mean that none of these things is transmissible or receivable as 'information'.

The case against the first alternative seems airtight. We do not have access to the decoding and encoding rules of others as 'information'. Their possession of such rules is, in this model, a precondition for their assimilation of information. We could not receive it. But this also means that there is no way, through ordinary coded communication, for new rules to be received. And therefore there is no way for our own coding rules to change. So the second alternative is the only acceptable one, and this alternative excludes the possibility of change in coding rules. Change, given this model, becomes impossible.

One can, of course, invent many variations on the 'code' analogy to account for change. Codes can be given levels of depth. If the primal code was sufficient to generate the code in which the change was made without complex new instructions, for example, the code might be changed on the basis of very little information. The message to change the code might be hidden in a code within the code. But in all these variations the basic problem remains. The message to change codes must be received, and it can only be received in a code that is already in the possession of the recipient.

Systems and closure

The solution to this problem is to escape the code metaphor. But the code metaphor is a means of expressing an idea that is much more difficult to let go of – the idea that our practices form a system that we cannot escape from. Because our practices are the sole means by which we have access to the world, we cannot change these means by reference to, for example, facts that are 'the unvarnished news of the world'. The only facts we have access to are those generated by our practices or constituted in terms of our presuppositions. Stanley Fish cites a series of assertions by Rorty, Goodman, Kuhn and himself, each with a message to the effect, as he quotes Rorty, 'that there is no way to think about either the world or our purposes except by using our language ... no way to break out of it by comparing it to something else'.[7] The quotations make the point that there is no way to compare our frame of reference to the 'external world'. Fish concludes his list with the comment that:

These are only representative formulations, and there are distinctions to be made between them, but I think it is fair to say that one consequence of following their general line is to make a problem out of change; for it is no longer possible to see change as occurring when the world or a piece of the world forces us to revise or correct our description of it; since descriptions of the world are all we have, change can only be understood as change in description, and we are left with the task of explaining not only how they come about, but why they should ever come about in the first place.[8]

He goes on to say that this is not the worst of it. If one locates practices, as he does, in 'the community', then 'there is insufficient distance ... [not only] between the community and the object of its attention; there is also insufficient distance between the community and its methods'. If the 'methods', the 'measures of adequacy and accuracy, are no less community- or paradigm-specific than the facts they are intended to measure, confirmation and validation would seem to be at once assured and empty'.[9]

Fish's solution to this problem is highly relevant to the puzzle with which this chapter began. He distinguishes between the practices or 'methods' of a community and its purposes, and argues that these stand in a kind of relationship in which change in general is not only possible but to be expected – but that not every change is possible. This is an important argument because it exemplifies a strategy that avoids the problems with which the chapter began. Change and persistence can be accounted for in Fish's conception because for him a culture (or the practices of an interpretive community) retains all the properties of unity and inaccessibility that are needed to account for persistence. He thus avoids the problematic idea that a set of fundamental rules which are not open to revision is imprinted on members of a community.

Fish draws an analogy with the mind. For the individual, he says, 'no beliefs *are* fundamental ... "the mind" is an assemblage of related beliefs any one of which can exert pressure on any other in a motion that can lead to a self-transformation'.[10] He then claims that this assemblage is never at equilibrium, and is thus the immanent source of change. Similarly for communities. Communities, like people, have assumptions, which include their 'self-conception' and 'the assumption of a relation between it and neighboring bodies of knowledge'. When something happens in a separate domain or discipline that affects belief *within* a particular interpretive community, it does so by virtue of these prior, embedded belief-like things:

When a community is provoked to change by something outside it, that something will already have been inside, in the sense that the angle of its notice – the angle by which it is related to the community's project even before it is seen – will determine its shape, not after it has been perceived, but *as* it is perceived. And all of this will follow from the community's understanding of itself as a mode of inquiry responsible to the facts and theorems of some, but not all, other modes of inquiry.[11]

These purposive (tacit!) givens, it appears, are something very close to 'fundamental assumptions' or the fundamental rules of a culture. But they are not rules – they are collective purposes.

As Fish describes interpretive communities, they are 'at once homogeneous with respect to some general sense of purpose or purview, and heterogeneous with respect to the variety of practices they can accommodate'.[12] Some people in the community may possess practices that others do not. This argument removes one major objection to the rules model of culture – we do not need to take everyone to be imprinted with the same rules. But it raises a question. The rules model was designed in part to explain how such things as persuasion are possible, and it explained the possibility of persuasion by the fact of the common possession of rules. Fish does not dispense with the idea of common possessions, but changes the item that is possessed. The practices themselves do not have to be 'shared', in this revised model – only the purposes which they serve have to be shared. Persuasion between the possessors of different interpretive practices is possible because each party has recourse to appeals to the common ground of shared purposes.

To be persuaded, an individual must be a member of an interpretive community and be persuaded according to its methods and its openings. But there is no persuasion outside of community practices and purposes, for even if a novel idea is conceived by an individual, the reception of this idea by other members of the community is constrained by these practices.[13] Change must be 'internal' in character.

How can collective purposes themselves change? Fish gives a mysterious answer to this, consistent with his characterization of the individual mind. He drops the notion that collective purposes are in some sense higher, prior, or more basic than practices. He says that 'there is no need to envision a point or goal outside of practice because practice is at every moment organized in relation to goals already known, although it should now go without saying that the accomplishment of these goals will be inseparable from the emergence of others and therefore inseparable from the call for more practice'.[14] Purposes and practices, then, beget or influence one another in a never-ending cycle of collective self-transformation. Purposes 'emerge'.

Fish gives some examples of cases where goals are revised in accordance with community practices or purposes. But in these cases, 'external' change is still ruled out. The body of 'internal' elements is more complex than the rules model of culture. He characterizes Wieder's 'convict code' with the comment that what we are dealing with 'is not a single simple organism, but a set of interlocking assumptions one of which can always be brought into play as a check against the others and all of which are answerable to the complex social situation that is at once the code's mooring and its accomplishment'.[15] Just as other 'assumptions' can be invoked, other 'concerns', internal to the activity, can be invoked. Such 'concerns' are presumably reflections of collective purposes.

Making the system (meaning the collective purposes, the community in which the purposes are rooted and which is defined by the purposes, together with the shared code and presuppositions, and the links between them) into something bigger and more complex than the original 'system' solves the problem of change in the following way. The relation of closure between these elements of the system remains – only the size and complexity of the system changes. The problem of change is solved by saying of any innovation or novel thing 'noticed' or message received that 'of course it is still internal to the system'. And the fact that the system is not entirely rigid, in the sense that it admits competing or conflicting practices, becomes the explanation of how change can occur – through the adjustment of relations between such 'internal' things as practices, collective purposes, and the kinds of facts that can be recognized and admitted by the practices. Change is limited, but only by the fact that 'this or that set of already in place concerns can (but not *must*) lead to the noticing and taking into account of an open-ended, although not infinite, range of phenomena'.[16]

'Open-ended, though not infinite' is an extremely weak formulation. If the notion of open-endedness is pushed too far, the notion of limitation is threatened, and with it the notion of system, for if there are no limits there is no system. 'Not infinite' still leaves a lot of space within which 'phenomena' can be noticed and taken into account. This brings us to the question of the nature of the limitation or closure in question. Fish could have argued that purposes are fundamental, and that purposes are therefore the source of the limits of possible noticings and accountings, but he did not, arguing that there was a dialectical rather than foundational relationship between these elements. We might gloss this appeal to dialectics, in at least one of its operational forms, as follows: practices

90 *Change and History*

may change in accordance with purposes and then produce 'noticings' that feed back to change purposes, perhaps by changing what is thought possible or real. There are no intrinsic limits to these processes, and this is a bit suspicious in itself, for it suggests that with these concessions Fish has given up the game entirely. In any case, 'noticing and taking into account' is not precisely to the point. In the code model, the stuff that is noticed or taken into account would be the information. How does one acquire new practices? If one says, as Fish does, that practices are at least partly tacit and inaccessible to us, the question of how they are acquired – the stumbling block of the last chapter – is still to be resolved.[17]

To answer the question of whether a meaningful notion of 'system' remains, it is worth considering what force, if any, this restriction has, and, correlatively, what sort of 'system' is established by the empirical evidence that exists that pertains to the phenomenon of closure. The second question, the question of what sort of 'system' is established by the facts, may be answered first. There are a number of classic formulations of the notion of, as Clifford Geertz puts it in a famous paper, 'common sense as a cultural system'. Geertz liberally employs the locutions discussed in Chapter 3 to make his case. 'Common sense is not what the mind cleared of cant spontaneously apprehends; it is what the mind filled with presuppositions... concludes.'[18] The examples are familiar – Zande magic, Navajo classification and so on – as is the lesson. Dramatic examples of variant classification schemes and the practical consequences of them are, indeed, an anthropological genre.

The most famous of these, E. E. Evans-Pritchard's study of the Azande, is a study of the imperviousness of belief in witchcraft to rational evidence or argument. Evans-Pritchard was thus able to describe elaborate rituals that had a central role in the life of the Azande, such as the giving of poison to certain birds and using the fact that they lived or died as a sign of the answer to queries put to them. The birds were not as Delphic as the Greek oracles: the Azande asked direct questions and sometimes got contradictory answers. But the Azande were nevertheless unshaken in their belief in the method. Zande informants simply did not demand complete understanding of witchcraft – they treated it as mysterious. But each conflict or inconsistency that Evans-Pritchard identified for his informants was explained away in *ad hoc* terms consistent with the idea of witchcraft.[19]

Other examples abound. Lévi-Strauss provides a dramatic account of death by sorcery, which is to say death through belief in a closed set of categories. The hypothesized medium of the effect was social. The person condemned by sorcery was treated by others 'as dead and an object of fear, ritual, and taboo', and this was supposed to be the proximate cause of death: physical integrity cannot withstand the dissolution of the social personality'.[20] But the account turns out to be not an ethnographic report, but hypothetical – a story of how a person *might* die as a consequence of becoming convinced, within the categories of magical reasoning, that he or she was to die.

The historian of religion Mircea Eliade gave the example of an Australian Aborigine group who carried around a pole which they regarded as the *axis mundi*, the connection between heaven and earth. When this pole was accidentally destroyed, they considered the connection between heaven and earth to have broken irretrievably, and lay down, as a group, to die.[21] The implications are similar.

The large conclusion to be drawn from these little anecdotes, and the famous and endlessly cited case of Zande magic, is that the 'system' of thought represented by Australian religious cosmology or Zande magic is complete and closed[22] – that these primitive thinkers were incapable, even in the face of imminent death through misconception, of noticing 'facts' obvious to us, the facts that if a stick breaks the world does not end, or that if a magical sign points in a certain way, death is not inevitable. But the drama of the stories does not make up for the fact that they do not match the claim of closure. Fish argues that what is 'not infinite' is the capacity for 'noticing and taking into account phenomena', which makes it seem that closure is a case of diminished capacity, and that the capacity of noticing is diminished by the 'set of already in place concerns' of the communities in question. But the evidence shows nothing about the capacity of the persons in question to notice hitherto unnoticed facts once they were pointed out, or even to notice them on their own – much less their capacity to learn new ways of thinking about the facts in question. It shows only, and at most, that these people failed to notice the facts that are obvious to us, or to think of them in ways other than the strange ways in which they apparently did think of them. Failures to notice are rather mundane errors of inattention or else the result of the *de facto* unavailability of alternative but learnable ways of thinking. They are not proofs of the *de jure* closure of a mental world. If the appropriate missionary had come on the scene when Eliade's Australians broke their pole, the story might have ended differently – for people can be taught, and sometimes taught very easily, to think in different ways and to notice and take into account hitherto unnoticed things.[23]

This gives us a kind of answer to the question of the force of the restrictions. The problem of transmission through codes, and the problem of change that is produced by the idea that what is received must be in the code that already exists, is replaced by a different problem. The sharp division between 'in the code' and 'not in the code' does not seem to hold for practices. They are allowed to change through other processes. Fish mysteriously calls these dialectical, meaning 'internal'. But it would be more reasonable to relax the notion that practices must be acquired 'in the code' and allow for the possibility of acquiring new practices from others more or less directly.

The facts we can bring to bear on this seem to fit this possibility – we change through demonstration effects, by copying or emulating externals, even though we cannot articulate the lessons we are seeing demonstrated in our own codes. But there do seem to be limits of various kinds on our capacity to understand and attend, and to accept novelty. What are they and what is their source?[24] To deal with these issues it would be best to dispose of another one: the distinction between primal acquisition and other forms. The significance of admitting the possibility of more or less direct acquisition of demonstrated practices is simply not clear. The other big fact of inaccessibility, the difficulty of getting access to other traditions, seems to be unaffected by this possibility: mastering, for example, the practices of koranic interpretation is not something that can be done directly.

Translations and abridgements

If we consider the possible forms of access to a tradition, a language, a conceptual scheme or a paradigm, we may distinguish between the primary mode, the mode in which persons initially acquire it, and a secondary mode, such as translation, reduction to explicit rules, or purely intellectual as opposed to embodied acquisition. Translation, one may claim, provides a kind of access to another tradition, but one that is restricted by the language into which the target language is translated. The important things about a primitive religion, for example, are necessarily lost in a translation to Christian or Christian-like terms or to the modern secular cosmology of science. 'Loss' accounts take various forms. Eliade claims that modern man has lost the religious sensibility necessary to grasp previous religious experience, and that consequently the world of early religion is simply closed off to him. Kuhn claims that there is an irreducible incommensurability between paradigms that makes full translation impossible. MacIntyre recommends learning a second tradition not through translation but 'as a first language'. Oakeshott distinguishes between 'abridgements' of a political tradition, such as the written American constitution or *laissez-faire* economic ideology, and the living, unwritten traditions which they attempt to reduce to a recipe.

What these accounts share is a thesis to the effect that something that is in some sense part of a tradition, paradigm or language is acquired by persons who gain access in the proper way, but is not acquired or transmitted in the other case. The thesis, then, rests on a notion of special transmission of the kind discussed in Chapter 4. The issue, in that chapter, was the transmission of the 'same' thing, and this notion was rejected as insupportable – or rather that a full development of the claim that some same substance was transmitted led to such outlandish theories as to lack minimal credibility. But if we drop the notions of sameness and substance, some sense can be given to the notion of differences that result from the causal history of acquisition, and through this some sense might be made of the apparent differences between acquisition by rule and by practice with which we began in Chapter 1. This in turn might yield an answer to the broader question of limitations on understanding or noticing.

One way to begin reconstructing this reasoning would be to distinguish between *practices*, meaning sets of individuated things which can be grasped, and *practice* or tradition conceived in a different way, as a more or less unitary but non-individuated thing. Oakeshott and T.S. Eliot, in their uses of the term tradition, appeal to the notion of a way of life that is something other than the additive product of a set of tacit rules. The term 'practice' similarly is sometimes used to denote a kind of unitary body that cannot be individuated into specific practices. *Mores* is certainly used by Sumner in this way in most connections, and *habitus* is used in this unindividuated way by Bourdieu. Even custom and habit as used by Hume can be interpreted in an unindividuated sense. The same contrast arises in interpreting Wittgenstein, in the form of the question of whether the notion of 'forms of life' is equivalent to the notion of a set of the same rules shared by a group.[25]

Making this distinction, however, is not the same as making sense of it. If a form of life is not a set of particular rules, or if a tradition is not a set of particular practices, what is it? Is it these things *together with* some other elements that are themselves non-mysterious, such as public shared performances? Or is a tradition or practice a new object that has new properties or new and mysterious elements, the product perhaps of combination or emergence? Fish gives an answer of the 'emergence' type when he appeals to the notions of collective purposes and of a collective body in which the practice inheres. But can practice be conceived without any appeal to such mysterious things?

Wittgenstein's comment that 'culture is an observance, or at least presupposes an observance' points to one solution to this problem. By 'culture' or 'form of life' we might mean a set – perhaps one that is not very well bounded or easy to give a specific identity to – of observances. We go to weddings and church services, boat races and schools, courts and voting booths. Eliot gave these kinds of activities as examples of what he meant by a 'culture'.[26] To participate in the observance in the appropriate way is a kind of sharing. The question is whether going through these performances is enough to participate in a tradition or way of life and possess it. Could one go through the observances and, so to speak, miss out on the way of life?

There is at least one school of thought which would insist that this was possible – that there is something in the blood that allows for the possibility of certain experiences, and that the culture would not be experienced in the same way by the person who lacked this inner quality – such as a Jew going to a performance of Wagner. And there are less inflammatory versions of this same thought. One might argue that it would require in one's background several generations of exposure to the appropriate observances to truly share in them. The 'spirit' of the observance, in this picture, would be something that, so to speak, seeped in with prolonged exposure, and the exposure of one or two generations is not sufficient. The observances themselves, in this case, would have a kind of power to produce the right spirit, but the power would be slow-acting and impossible to open oneself sufficiently to in one lifetime, or as an adult. Being 'to the manner born' is essential, but being born to one who is 'to the manner born' is possibly not.

There is something to the *thought* behind the picture, if not the picture itself. A familiar illustration, and indeed one that is central to the literature on political traditions, concerns the question of whether the forms of democracy are sufficient to produce democratic politics in the absence of a specific democratic political tradition. The question, as it was typically put in the nineteenth century, was whether some desirable political system, such as limited monarchy with parliamentary rule, could be imitated by countries without Anglo-Saxon traditions. The same question arises today in much the same form with respect to liberal democracy in the third world. It arose for Austin, as we have seen, with respect to the lower classes in nineteenth-century Britain, and to the American sociologists of the turn of the century with respect to immigrants from the south of Europe.

Oakeshott's formulation of the problem is the following. Political traditions cannot be acquired from books or formulae. The thing that is enacted in regimes that take over British constitutional forms as they have been 'abridged' into explicit rules are taking over a different thing from what the British themselves possess. And the difference is necessitated by the act of abridgement, the making of a matter of rule what is for the British a matter of practice.[27]

The picture we get here is that there is a contrast between doing something by virtue of the possession of a tradition and by following a rule book. But this is a contrast that runs into a series of difficulties that arise from an ambiguity in senses of the concept of tradition itself. We may distinguish between two uses of the concept of tradition. One may be called the analytic use, and it figures particularly in certain kinds of explanations, such as the explanation of the descent of particular ideas. The other may be called the contrastive or pejorative use, and it figures in passages like Oakeshott's which deny that some particular activity is done in accordance with a tradition or that some particular group possesses a tradition of a given kind.[28]

The analytic use may be illustrated by the example of feminism. It might be said that feminism is a revolt against the tradition of patriarchy. It might be added to this that it is a revolt against tradition as such, or against all existing traditions, because all the existing traditions of our societies are patriarchal in character. The analytic user of the concept of tradition would reply to this by noticing that the appeal of feminism has to do in the first instance with an ideal that is imported from politics, namely the ideal of egalitarianism. This ideal is itself the product of a tradition, the tradition of formal equality or confraternity among limited groups of males, which was transposed to the political realm as the idea of male suffrage, and subsequently extended to the idea of universal suffrage. The feminist idea that not merely suffrage restrictions, but the law, language, practices of representation, and market economies are forms of the repression of women is an extension of the idea of equality into new applications. The original transposition of equality into politics provided an alternative to what appeared, on reflection and comparison, to be the unjustifiably hierarchical character of existing society. Feminism then extended the idea of equality from the political realm to the private and domestic one. But each step in this process was one in which a tradition was being employed. At no point was tradition as such,

96 *Change and History*

or even the whole of existing traditions, repudiated; rather, one tradition, the egalitarian, was employed against, and enabled the problematization of and reflection on, other traditions.

These 'transpositions' or applications to a new field might be thought not to qualify as cases of continuity in traditions, and this raises again the whole question of the location of tradition and the problem of sameness or identity. If they do not qualify because there is some essence to the tradition of egalitarianism, the question arises as to what these essences are and, if the essential stuff is partly hidden or tacit, how it is transmitted. This returns us to the problems of transmission discussed in the last chapter without solving them. One might avoid these problems by rejecting the idea of essences and the idea that sameness depends on occult transmissions. In the case of egalitarianism, at least, it is arguable that continuity can be established by considering public utterances and uses of concepts. The fact that extensions of the concept of equality to new uses are intelligible to persons who use and understand the term in its previous uses suffices to establish the continuity of the tradition and thus its 'identity'. This is a criterion to which we will return, for it suggests a solution to Fish's problem of the limits of a tradition.

The contrastive use of the concept of tradition provides what appears to be a quite different kind of answer to the question of whether egalitarianism is a tradition. In terms of the concepts we have been discussing here, to say that something is not a tradition, or is not backed by a tradition, is to say that there is no tacit shared object – no presuppositions or *mores* – in the appropriate relation to the activity in question. Needless to say, the epistemic character of such claims is a mystery – how precisely one determines whether or not something is backed by a tradition is never stated by those who use the term in this way. But if we explore some possible senses of 'no tradition' claims, we can get an idea of what is at stake.

If the mark of a traditional activity is its inaccessibility without special initiatory training, inaccessibility through translation alone, the lack of a tradition can be thought of as transparency or universal accessibility, or the lack of barriers to acquisition. If practices are thought to be the sorts of things that are applied and change tacitly in application, and if the changes are thought to be transmitted along with the explicit parts of the tradition rather than being learned from scratch by each person, then the lack of a tradition may be thought of as the case in which there is no transmission of the results of the experience of application. One might imagine, for example, do-it-yourself carpentry done exclusively from books, such that each person who used the book learned for him- or herself how to hammer a nail or start a cut with a saw, rather than learning this from another person who had mastered the skill. Another use of the notion of 'no tradition' is related to this: an unrealized ideal, such as radical egalitarianism may be said to not be a tradition or at least not a tradition of practice because there has been no case in which the ideal has been successfully applied to produce a form of life. Presumably this last clause means not simply that no one or no group has attempted successfully to live in accordance with these ideals, but that the learnings from past applications of the ideal have not been passed on to successive persons in such a way that the continuity and character of the form of life is something more than that which would be the result of continued reference to the explicit ideal and new 'information' and experience alone.

It is difficult to see how to avoid some notion of an inaccessible added element by virtue of which there is continuity. So we are faced with Hobson's choice. We may accept the concept of tradition, but only by bearing the burden of the problematic notion of transmission of some sort of tacit stuff. But the easy identification of the missing stuff with a specially transmitted common tacit object is itself open to objection. It is possible to think that the thing added to the explicit rules, or the thing which enables a person to perform more or less successfully in concert with others, is individual or private, rather than transmitted in the problematic sense of a tacit rule or as tacit knowledge. It is also possible to think of the unindividuated body of practice on which an activity rests as being composed not of some sort of mysterious collective object but of these individual additions to what is explicit and public, such as writings and utterances and 'observances'. It is far from clear that there is any historical fact of the matter that can distinguish between the two hypotheses. What are the implications of thinking of these added things in a tradition as individual rather than collective?

Emulations and habits

If the passing on of something that is irreducible to explicit rules is the mark of a tradition, it might be argued that the fact that one can emulate an activity, for example on a computer, by supplying explicit, mechanical rules, suggests that a tradition consisting of these rules exists and is somehow transmitted to or otherwise individually acquired by persons who are able to participate in and perform the activities in question.

'Knowledge engineering' is the branch of learning that attempts to 'elicit' the kind of information from people which enables such emulative machines to be constructed. The success of a knowledge-engineering effort shows that there is something necessary in the way of 'knowledge' in order to perform certain tasks beyond the previously articulated rules.

But the implications of the success of a knowledge-engineering effort are not entirely helpful to the thesis of transmittable tacit knowledge. The knowledge engineer starts out with an explicitly defined task which is to be emulated. The machines on which the emulation is to occur may differ quite dramatically from the body of the person who is supplying the knowledge to be engineered – for example a robot replacing a lathe-operator's body together with a traditional mechanical lathe. The lathe-operator obviously does not possess the 'knowledge' to run the robot's body. The lathe-operator's embodied achievements and powers (to perform a specific range of tasks) are what is being emulated. So the knowledge that is identified by the knowledge engineer is not, so to speak, the tacit contents of the mind of the lathe-operator, but suggestions that enable him or her to emulate a particular human performance on a robot – to produce, that is, a set of instrumentally useful rules that, for the task in question, produce the 'same' results. 'Sameness' here is of course not a natural category, but something defined relative to the purposes of the emulation itself.

In this case something – a computer-driven robot – is emulating an activity, but obviously not literally following the same rules. But if something – a machine driven by a computer – that is not following the same rules can emulate, why can't this same kind of relationship, of emulation, occur between persons? Why not suppose that the performances of an individual can emulate those of another sufficiently to pass for adequate or competent without the person possessing any internal thing, such as tacit knowledge, that is the same as what the other person possesses? We can also suppose, quite safely, that the individual could habitualize these emulations, so that such individualized possessions persist in the individual.

If we take this process of emulation to be a possible substitute for transmission, the issue in connection with the historical concept of practice changes, as do all the issues that arise in connection with the notion of the persistence of *mores* and the historical reality of tradition as fact. The basic issue is this. The idea of the special persistence of *mores* or traditions was thought to necessitate the hypothesis of the existence and transmission of some sort of collective object. But there is no need for any such collective object. The same kinds of persistence can occur entirely through individual (and possibly literally different) habits that arise in the individual as a *consequence* of the emulative performance of particular activities, observances and the like. Raising the possibility is enough to undermine the notion of traditions as hidden collective object-like possessions, the appeal of which rests on the supposed explanatory necessity of the existence of some such object.

In each case of a supposed tradition, there is a myriad of observances, statements to be understood, acts to perform and respond to, and so forth. All these things are 'public'. In each case the same question arises. Is it possible to do the things that make one a participant in this body of activities without possessing the hidden collective part of it, the tradition or practice? If the answer is yes, the criteria for possession of the tradition or practice must be separable from the facts of performance themselves; otherwise there is no fact of the matter to possession. If the answer is no, the issue comes down to a causal one, and the choice is between the hypothesis of a hidden collective fact, with all its problems about transmission, and some other hypothesis or set of hypotheses, such as the hypothesis that the observances, performances and actions themselves form the relevant *individual* habits.

The character of practices, or practice, as a historical object, as we have seen, is elusive. We began the chapter with a problem analogous to the problem of anomalous rapidity of the acquisition of grammar, namely the problem of the anomalous persistence of *mores*. This is a dubious problem in the first place – anomalousness is a comparative notion. To be an anomaly literally means to be out of accordance with some law. In this case it is not clear what prior expectations about cultural change are being violated by the persistence of *mores*, or what expectations we are entitled to. Yet there are some real issues here. People do not, as Sumner noted, change their sentiments and conduct in the way they might if their ideas were like a theory of the world, with logical connections between the parts of the theory such that the explicit acceptance of a changed premiss leads directly to changed conclusions and changed actions. But the connection of such facts with persistence is not clear. It is not clear, for example, that this kind of persistence cannot be accounted for without recourse to the idea of some sort of collective causal object, such as the *mores*.

If acting in accordance with a tradition is acting in accordance with the way of life of a community, and if the way of life of a community includes certain observances, performances and activities, and individual habits and mental habits arise through engaging in the relevant performances, nothing need follow with respect to the causal role or status of practice understood as a kind of collective fact. All that need follow is this: by performing in certain ways, people acquire habits which lead them to continue to perform, more or less, in the same ways. The observances, so to speak, cause *individual* habits, not some sort of collectively shared single habit called a practice or a way of life, which one may possess or fail to possess. If this is so, the collective or public facts about traditions or 'cultural systems of meaning' begin and end with the observances or public objects themselves. Everything else is individual – there is no collective tacit fact of the matter at all.

The arguments I have presented in this chapter are exclusively negative. They are a response to a particular kind of claim, a claim to the effect that some notion of tradition as a collective non-public fact is necessitated by the legitimate historical uses of the term and its cognates. The claim is difficult to contest simply in this negative way, however. One inevitably uses terms, such as 'way of thinking', that appear to be interpretable only in terms of the idea of a hidden collective fact. And inevitably one is forced to supply alternative possible explanations of at least bits of the processes or phenomena that are central to the past uses of the terms. To say that observances are the cause of habits rather than their result, however, suggests that one could give a more elaborate account of the processes by which observances continue: give a positive alternative to go along with the case against tradition, tacit knowledge and 'presupposition'.

The demand for a positive picture to go along with the negative arguments needs to be distinguished from the demand for adequate negative arguments. From what I have said in the last two chapters, it should be clear that I think the case for practices, or practice, understood as a hidden collective object, is faced with such serious difficulties with respect to the means of the transmission and acquisition of these objects that it cannot be accepted, and that appeals to 'practice' used in this sense, either in philosophy or social theory, are therefore appeals to nothing. But I accept that it is difficult to see the implications of this point. In the next chapter I shall provide the rudiments of an alternative picture of the phenomena covered by the idea of practice, and a few suggestions about what social theory can and cannot be if we accept the negative arguments. I shall also provide the beginnings of an answer to the question of what sorts of philosophical problems one can address if one accepts these negative arguments, and what sorts of projects are ruled out by them.

6
The Opacity of Practice

The role of practice as a concept, and of its cognates, such as tacit knowledge and presupposition, is to make good an insufficiency. The insufficiency takes various forms, and the appeal to practices serves various purposes, only a few of which have been discussed here. In Chapter 1, I concentrated on the philosophical reasons for appealing to the concept. But the concept, I suggested, was itself non-philosophical, and appealing to it only served philosophers' purposes *because* practices could be treated as substantial facts. In later chapters, I discussed the various conceptions of these facts that have emerged in the domain of their most self-conscious explanatory uses, primarily in social theory.

But the implications of the argument go beyond social theory and philosophy. The same relation, of an insufficiency made good by appeal to the concept of practice or one of its cognates, holds in many other domains, such as the law. The problem that gives rise to the appeal to tacit knowledge in law is the problem of getting judicial decisions out of books of laws. The act is performed with a higher degree of consistency among the trained and experienced than the untrained and inexperienced. But it requires knowledge, or something like knowledge, that is itself not in any books or sets of explicit rules. Rudolph von Ihering had appealed to the notion of a 'judicial sense' arising from experience in order to account for judges' abilities to do so. Today, tacit legal knowledge is a practical problem for artificial intelligence practitioners attempting to model legal reasoning.[1]

Norms are 'societal'; *Sitten* inhere in a *Volk*. Lawyer and judge are 'social' rather than natural categories. And in the case of other insufficiencies analogous to those that arise in relation to the law, the same pattern holds. The knowledge in question is localized to some group. In the closely related case of constitutions, the problem takes the following form: written constitutions, or written abridgements of unwritten constitutions, have different results when they are enacted in states which have 'different political traditions' or in which people have different habits of dealing with one another as citizens – therefore written constitutions are insufficient in practice and insufficient to explain political diversity. Ethics is subject to the same kind of insufficiency, which becomes apparent in the face of the problem of the diversity of morals. The kinds of accounts of moral conduct, upbringing and the like that we use in practical moral reasoning in our own societies do not suffice to account for or make sense of the behaviour of those in other societies – what we take to be depraved, they take to be normal, or even to be obligatory or good. We account for the differences by identifying or adverting to 'practices' that they share and we lack, or that we share and they lack.

In other cases the insufficiency arises from purely intellectual considerations. We cannot interpret the writings of past times unless we take account of the different 'assumptions' made by past writers. Sometimes the problem arises from our theory of interpretation or our epistemology. If we suppose that theory is underdetermined by data, or that texts are open to an infinite range of interpretations, we are faced with the problem of making sense of interpretive or scientific texts which take for granted something opposed to it – that given data determine particular theories or that a given text is open to only one interpretation, or to certain favoured interpretations.

In each of these cases the idea of a tacit common possession, something that is itself not a text, fact or event – a 'hidden collective object' shared among a certain set of persons – seems to be a plausible hypothesis. The plausibility depends on analogies to 'public' things, like articulated beliefs, facts and texts. The terms for this kind of collective non-public possession, such as tacit knowledge, rely directly on these analogies. The non-public things have effects or causal powers like those of things that are themselves explicit and public.

Doing without practice

The fact that a crucial step in using these analogies is made in terms of 'social' categories places these accounts in a special relationship with social theory. The distribution of these objects is most readily understood in terms of categories like group, society and so forth, as Fish's term 'interpretive community' suggests. Indeed, so close is the relation between the concepts of tradition, tacit knowledge and the like, and the concepts we employ in talking about social life, that the terms employed are sometimes, as in the case of Hume's use of 'custom', simply borrowed from one vocabulary and used in the other.

But to grant the existence of such things as *Weltanschauungen*, tacit knowledge, *Sitte* with causal powers, paradigms and so forth is to create an epistemic and explanatory problem for the social theorist. What sorts of objects are these? How can they be known, how can their causal properties be assessed, and how do they change? These are just the beginnings – the more we look into the answers, the more questions arise. How do these peculiar things get from one person to another? Where are they located? How does the same thing get 'reproduced' in different people? What sort of sameness or identity is at stake here? Does the sameness necessary for speaking historically of the identity of 'traditions', for example, correspond to some sameness-preserving feature of the transmission or acquisition of a tradition? Or is the historian's sameness purely the historian's imposition?

The answers to these questions, as we have seen, vary. None of them turn out well at all. The epistemic problem with the notions of presupposition and tradition is that these are unusual objects. To make a very long discussion very short, the problem with them is this. They present themselves as natural objects, with natural powers. But the only access we have to them is through our own 'culture'. From the point of view of what we can know about them, or how we can construct them, they are irremediably cultural facts. We need a starting point *within* culture or practice to recognize something else *as* practice. Without comparisons between our practices and theirs we will mistakenly place the differences we see into the category of natural, in the category of first- rather than second-nature or treat them as individual variations, or simply fail to recognize a practice as a practice. So the very constitution of a practice as an object is tainted by our starting point, which is itself a contingent fact which we can neither understand nor overcome. We are indeed locked within our horizons in this respect. We cannot distinguish nature from culture on a basis beyond culture, except perhaps as a result of what I have called a scientific miracle, such as the discovery of a grammar gene, which might enable us to separate the genetic part of, say, our linguistic practices from the cultural part.

104 *The Opacity of Practice*

These difficulties are not fatal – epistemic problems abound in social theory. But the difficulty in conceiving of these objects is more serious than the difficulty in deciding when or where they apply. The major constraint on the concept of 'shared practices' derives from the notion of 'sharing'. The problem of how the same thing gets into different people is entailed by the idea that different people possess the same practice. If the notion of sameness is dropped, however, the concept collapses into habit – into a non-public, non-collective fact.

But dropping the notion of 'same practices' seems to cause new problems. My discussion of the epistemic issues itself relied on the notion of practice or culture. So if the notion is abandoned, my epistemic discussion begs the question of what a culture is in the first place. Moreover, it might be argued that the problem of distinguishing nature and culture is itself a fake. Everything, this line of argument might go, is a 'construction', including scientific miracles. Hence everything is a matter of culture after all – there is no escape from our practices of representation even on the level of our reflexive understanding of our own practices of representation. So the attempt to make the notion of practice into something more than a construction was doomed in the first place.

With this, however, we arrive at a real muddle – perhaps even at the heart of darkness. What sort of claim is 'everything is constructed' if there is no contrast between constructed and unconstructed, between nature and culture? What sort of claim is 'the concept of practice is itself a construction'? This is on the one hand a philosophical problem, for the notion of practice appears to lead back to itself as a source of contradiction, in which the claim rests upon a distinction that the claim denies. On the other hand, it is a problem that needs to be faced at the place of its origin – in the realm of social theory. Whatever revisions of the concept we are forced to make in the face of its difficulties in social theory will bear on its unreflective uses as a boundary to philosophical discourse or as a resource for literary theory. Practice as a concept and the appeal to it may have to go. The backstop may be simply taken away, and the problems it solved may need to be readdressed in new terms.

If society is *not* made up, Durkheim says, of representations, or representations and practices, could it be 'made up' of something else, or rather could the things we formerly explained by reference to these hidden collective things, be explained differently? Could observances, performances, utterances (and all the other sorts of things that people notice, understand, respond to and, in the course of doing so, form habits) be what 'makes up' society? What if we say this: there are no hidden collective objects; there is, however, a large body of private mental traces – what I have called habits – which persist and which enable people to emulate and operate in relation to one another. These mental traces, however, are effectively opaque to analysis. They are individual, private and, as best we can tell, irremediably diverse. It is only on the surface – in the forms of expression that others can, more or less successfully, respond to – that there is any kind of uniformity to them. The only mutuality we have or can have is the result of the acquisition of habits that enable us to more easily get on with others. We often fail to do this, or fail in particular domains. There is no sameness other than the sameness of effects – no hidden sameness to explain overtly similar performances.

The opacity of practice, if we accept this image, is not simply a result of the epistemic problems of disentangling the natural from the cultural (a problem which arises also for distinguishing different strands of culture, that is, distinct practices, from one another) but a feature of the causal properties of the stuff to which we have applied the term 'practice'. If what we have are private habits, with a variegated causal structure, that arise in response to public things, there is nothing to be learned about them beyond the summary description of practice in terms of its overt manifestations, because there is nothing there – nothing non-individual, that is.

Much of what we thought we knew about practices is unchanged if we accept this revised picture. The truth in Sumner is this: whatever ensemble of experiences produces the habits that people have, and that lead to the persistence of what appear to us to be similar forms of behaviour, is beyond our powers to determine or to manipulate very effectively. The reason stateways fail to modify folkways is that policy-makers often get it wrong – the experiences the state manipulates are not the experiences that produce the habits that produce the visible patterns they seek to change. By the same token, we may manipulate experiences in ways that form habits – this is after all what education is – without understanding what habits we are producing and how they will later manifest themselves. The observances we choose to enforce on children in order to teach honesty or respect for others may instead teach cheating and disrespect for others. And if the habits that are formed by the experiences particular children may have outside the school, during the times they are not participating in an enforced observance, such as a supervised game, are habits that make it easier for them to play the game as an occasion for cheating and disrespect, the game will not have the same habit-producing effects as it does for other children.

106 The Opacity of Practice

The conclusion we arrived at in the last chapter, that there could be no difference between the tacit part of common practices of a people and the habits induced by participation in the same observances, thus has no special practical value as a guide to manipulation. We have a good notion that the habits formed, for example, in games are carried over into other areas of life. Wellington's remark that the battle of Waterloo was won on the playing fields of Eton, or General Groves' belief that Leo Szilard could not be relied upon because he had never played baseball, are both bits of homespun sociology that might be true. But we don't know, and can't determine, what the relevant ensemble of observances for the production of given desirable habits consists of. Even the routines of inmates of a total institution, such as a prison or mental hospital, routines that are purposely limited and purposely designed to induce new habits, contain observances that form the 'wrong' habits, habits contrary to those that the governors and theorists of these institutions intended to be formed, because they can be interpreted or 'played' in a way alien to these intentions.

The power to transform habits through enforced observances is limited because observances are open to other interpretations. Successful performances can be brought off – emulated without detection or indeed without a person's having any sense that they have got the observance or the performance wrong – by persons whose habits differ from one another and by persons who lack the desired habits. But some observances and performances have a more compelling power: they seem to entrap participants, and preclude 'multiple interpretations'. One cannot get a degree in physics, or a Jesuit education, without acquiring some deeply rooted intellectual allegiances and mental habits along the way. The idea of deeply rooted allegiances is itself deeply rooted. One thing that we can reasonably infer from the everyday knowledge we do have about habits is this: the time and order of the acquisition of habits has some bearing on the difficulty of acquiring new habits and there is a kind of natural economy of habits such that some habits cannot be acquired without displacing others. It is plausible to suppose, for example, that some basic habits of affection and attachment that are conditions for the success of adult affections and attachments are established in the world of the very young child, and that these habits of affection differ between people in quite significant ways. Psychotherapists deal with such habits and try to get people to unlearn existing habits and learn new ones.

The prior acquisition of given habits may preclude the acquisition of others, or shape what kinds of 'emulation' of the performances of other people is possible. Thus it may be, as Eliade argued, that we have lost the capacity for religious experience of earlier times. It may be that no amount of translation, emulation or interpretive effort will enable us to bridge the gap. The reason for this, to borrow Veblen's phrase, may be 'trained inability' – something that cannot be set aside, as the phenomenologists thought could be done with presuppositions, but which we can at best unlearn and replace. And the practical possibility of doing this may be nil. This feature of habit formation thus explains the difference between first and second acquisitions of a tradition, as well as the inaccessibility of some cultures. But the point holds within 'cultures' as well – there is no guarantee that the habits of affection and attachment of our neighbours will ever be intelligible to us or congruent with ours.

The difficulty of acquiring the habits necessary to be proficient at one kind of performance or observance without having previously mastered another kind of observance or performance is a basic 'empirical' fact that fits with the 'habits' model. The causal link that the facts point to – between past habits and present difficulties or ease in the acquisition of habits – can serve as a substitute for some of the causal links that social theorists have traditionally been concerned with. We may suppose that there are circular links between observances, the habits they induce and abilities to acquire new habits. To take Spranger's example, the Christian life may come more easily to those who have come to be habituated to a particular set of observances. It will seem natural for them to take certain steps – easier for them to acquire the habits that will make them able to enact a Christian life, have the inner experiences that other Christians report and empathize with other Christians' expressions of their inner experiences.

Differences in prior habits are a potential source of differences in interpretations and understandings of the 'same' public objects, such as actual texts, rituals and the like. What one sees in, and takes away from, a given 'observance' – visiting the Vietnam War Memorial in Washington, for example – will potentially be different depending on the prior experiences one brings to the task of interpreting it and interpreting one's response to it. Obviously the relevant experiences and effects will vary in virtually every respect between persons going to this monument, and consequently the habits of mind produced or changed by the experience of making sense of it and of one's emotional response to it will differ. Nevertheless, experiences, observances, performances and habits may fit together in a kind of self-perpetuating causal whole. Sheer redundancy of experience within a society may enforce a considerable degree of consistency in overt manifestations of habits. The causes appealed to here – the habit-producing effects of observances and performances and the predisposing effects of habits (and therefore understandings) on the acquisition of new habits (and understandings) – may be very powerful. Durkheim of course was impressed by the idea that there were such self-perpetuating causal wholes or circles, and supposed that one could make some sort of more precise theoretical sense out of them. The existence of such bodies of observances raises a crucial question. Is 'hegemonic power' of the sort that resides in a set of observances possible?

Power, reason and reality

The appeal of such thinkers as Foucault rested in large part on the answer they gave to this question. The compelling power of such systems had previously been explained (or self-explained within the system) as a matter of reason, natural truth and the like. The systems could be reinterpreted as 'conventional' or 'ideological' on the grounds of the fact of historical variability and change. Episodes of change, in which the ideological character of a given set of practices had not yet become hidden, could be identified, and the explicit expressions of ideology could be used as a guide to the hidden ideology that subsequently perpetuated itself tacitly. The 'practices' could then be reassigned from the category 'reason' to the category 'convention' and one could account for the convention in terms of the hidden intentions behind the practices. Ordinary intentions are made possible by the practices. The determination of the hidden intentions behind the perpetuation of the system is a matter of determining who benefits. One consequence of this reasoning is that 'power' loses its contrastive force – everything is reducible to it; the other is that ideology loses its contrastive force. Moreover, in the end they reduce to the same thing: power/knowledge techniques which empower and disempower.

What I have argued here parallels this series of steps, but comes to a different end, so it is perhaps worthwhile to mark the differences. The key to what I have argued is this: there is no 'system' in the sense of a commonly possessed non-public object. There are only individual habitualizations. Where does this leave us with such questions as power? A related question can be asked with respect to intellectual systems, such as mathematics, which seem to have a coherence and 'reality' that cannot be treated as 'no more than convention', much less 'no more than individual habit'. The difficulty for the picture I have been presenting here is that these systems seem to have a special autonomy and deserve some sort of special explanation which acknowledges this autonomy. But on the account given here, there is no room for such an explanation. The 'systems' of mathematics and hegemonic 'power' obviously differ. But they represent the extreme points at which 'anti-systematic' accounts are liable to fail. I will take them up in turn.

Mathematics

What accounts for the phenomenological sense of the reality and autonomy of the truths of mathematics? The way to begin with this problem is to recognize that the phenomenological sense often errs. Medieval thinkers were as fully convinced of the miraculous and cognitively probative character of such things as the agreements they found between the numbers of elements in their various classificatory schemes as we are of the miraculous agreements between mathematics and physical phenomena. But having said this, there is the fact of the phenomenological sense itself to contend with. Why do we even think that mathematical objects are 'real'?

When we acquire habits through 'practice' there is a process of feedback; being able to go on successfully provides various rewards, and perhaps even its own rewards. Doing mathematics – whether comprehending the steps in a proof or mastering addition – consists in large part of coming to think in ways that enable one to go on more easily, or to go on to additional steps. Inability to go on, to emulate the steps or procedures, is a sign of failure in comprehension. In mathematics these signs are generally visible – at least it is difficult to go on erroneously and continue to get results that square with expectations, with other procedures for getting what should be the same results and with the results that others get. What we may call unconscious learning, that is to say, the acquisition of habits (and powers of prediction or expectations), occurs *in the course of* understanding a proof.

The same kind of acquisition occurs in the course of reading a book or interpreting a text. And in learning mathematics we face the same kind of problem we face in mastering a text: we must, to 'go on successfully', in each of these domains, form the habits that enable us to do so. In these cases, of course, a variety of experiences may go into the shaping of our habits – experiences with the material as well as experiences with others, such as being corrected, or criticized, or faced with an alternative

110 The Opacity of Practice

interpretation. But in the end the successes and the sense of what comes next or should come next are ours. This is the basis of our phenomenological sense of the autonomy of the objects of these habits – of the stuff that seems for us to hold together the observances and performances that our habits enable us to succeed in.

The stuff is not reducible to 'convention' because our mastery is not only the mastery of the responses of others. But it is also not reducible to the 'real world' because the habits could not have been formed without the experiences of the interventions of other people. In the case of physics, the 'real world' by itself underdetermines the habits we form. In the case of mathematics there is underdetermination too, in the sense that there are other ways to go on – by quaddition rather than addition, for example. But we cannot decide whether we employ one and not the other because of the innate structure of the mind or because the people around us do. Deciding this question would require the kind of nature–culture disentanglement that we have seen to be epistemically out of reach.

What we can say is this. Kripke's Wittgenstein is right to think that the freedom that exists on the level of explicit rule-making or theory, in this case the freedom to invent and follow a mathematical rule that conforms to the series 2, 4, 6, 8 and goes on in a way that is consistent with this rule but does not produce 10, 12, 14 as immediate successors, is illusory. Finding rules that can continue a series differently is a game, and an easy one. Acquiring the habit of continuing the series as others do and going on in ways that they recognize as correct is a different matter. Inventing ways of going on that others can themselves learn by emulation and so replace their earlier habits is yet another. The latter two cases are constrained, though not as a consequence of the existence of some sort of group ethic, but rather by the fact that anyone who actually habitually counted in a way that continued the series differently would be baffled by the simplest activities, such as giving change or finding street addresses, not to mention other more difficult emulative tasks, such as following the solutions of problems in higher mathematics or mimicking these solutions in novel cases, in a world of people who had different habits which enabled them to emulate one another easily. They may also be constrained by properties of the brain, which dispose us to form habits in some ways and not others – properties that might be revealed by the discovery of a 'maths gene' or by matching anomalies in maths-learning with biological anomalies.

Nothing in the situation described here requires an appeal to 'system' or mathematical reality in the sense of a hidden collective object transmitted socially. There is in general no way to make a distinction between 'having habits that enable public proficiency' and 'possessing some shared thing on the basis of which proficiency is possible'. The only test of 'possession of a shared thing' is proficiency, and this can be the only test. There is no reason to believe that others have different habits unless there is an occasion that reveals this. And one can learn that one was 'taking something differently all along' only by learning a new way to take something and seeing that this enables one to be more proficient or better able to emulate the publicly displayed proficiencies of others. But one can also never arrive at the knowledge that one *is* 'taking things in the same way' – except in the sense of proficiently managing the same public performances.

Power

Systems of power, as they have usually been understood, rely on routines – paradigmatically routines of obedience. They are 'reasonless routines', reasonless in the sense that the system of power depends, in a practical way, on obedience in accordance with routines without separate justifications of commands.[2] The routines are thus givens. They can be resisted or overthrown, but only with great difficulty. There is a difference between 'routines' that are explicit, about which there are beliefs, such as beliefs in their legitimacy, and which can be backed by force, and 'routines' that are, so to speak, tacit. Persuasion, for example, can be said to depend on these routines. Political culture distributes power by conferring it on those who are in a position to employ these tacit routines. The routines that make up a system of power are thus like a stick, but a stick with two unequal ends. Because they are hidden, these routines are inaccessible to reform and often frustrate it – and thus are a more profound basis of power than naked force. Indeed, the employment of force itself, and of other explicit forms of power, depends on the following of routines. In the face of this kind of 'hegemonic' power, re-education or re-culturation is necessary.

Two points need to be made about this picture. The first is that the fact that practices confer advantages to some at the expense of others is a truism. *Any* set of politically relevant habits is a stick which can be grasped more effectively on one end than another, and more effectively on the 'power' end by some people that others. The ability to persuade, impress and inspire, no less than the ability to physically coerce, are distributed unevenly. What is at issue is whether there is something mysterious about the perpetuation of a specific system of practices that reproduces these relative advantages. In one sense, there is no mystery. Perpetuation of systems is of course *intentionally* aimed at by political agents who benefit from the systems. There are of course many relevant intentions, and the intended consequences of intentional action may bring about the same result. Parents may choose to equip their children for a world in which power and advantage take particular known forms, thus 'reproducing' the forms by keeping them supplied with persons competent to employ them. Policy-makers may prefer to preserve arrangements that are known to benefit particular groups or types. But if intentions sufficed to explain the facts of system perpetuation, there would be no need to appeal to hidden systematic causes. The issue is whether there is some such cause or purpose, something like 'group interests' that have explantory power beyond the conscious intentional decisions of individuals, or which explain their conscious intentional decisions.

The intentions of 'class fractions' and the like must be inferred from the causal process in which they play an explanatory role. The ends, that is, the perpetuation of advantage, are inferred from the selection of 'means', that is, the practices that produce advantages. If practices stay the same, they stay the same because of the quasi-intention of the advantaged to perpetuate them. The secret complicity of the disadvantaged in the perpetuation of the rules that disadvantage them is the real core of power. Identifying the practices of reproduction that perpetuate disadvantage is the first step to overcoming the practices – or so this reasoning goes. And there is a compelling 'empirical' fact of persistent advantage that can be accounted for in these terms.

If, as I have suggested, we dispense with the idea of a hidden process of 'reproduction', where are we left with the fact of relations of power and the persistence of disadvantage? Nothing I have said here denies the existence of culture in the sense of a body of observances, performances and the like – public things – and a body of habitual learnings, perhaps different in various ways for each individual, but which can collectively amount to a stick which it is more advantageous to hold on one end than another, and which some people can seize more easily than others. The 'reproduction' of the culture, however, is a separate matter. The reason it is hidden, or so I would claim, is that there is no such process. The process of learning and acquiring the habits that enable one to go on in life, and the fact that some of the habits thus acquired are more or less consistent and predictable within social groups, makes people subject to 'manipulation'. Some people, to put it simply, will be better able to get what they want, given *any* such set of more or less congruent and predictable individual habits. Because the habits persist, advantage persists.

A political culture, it might be added, is not itself subject to ready manipulation precisely because of the individualized character of what is learned. The relevant habits are not all acquired at once, or in the same place. But there is considerable redundancy in the 'lessons' one learns about power, from one's first spanking to one's last encounter with a committee, so it is perhaps unsurprising that they cannot be easily unlearned. The reason the process seems hidden is precisely that there is no magic moment at which the lessons are learned, and no single point at which they are 'transmitted'. There is, needless to add, no single hegemonic quasi-intention behind these lessons. They are part and parcel of the lessons of life, and are no more and no less subject to control.

Social theory

This general picture, containing individual habits, public performances and public observances, might be treated as a rudimentary new social theory. Moreover, it might be elaborated in various ways that would bring this picture closer to traditional social theory. The image of the body of habits as a stick with unequal ends might be elaborated, for example. But the main implication of the picture presented here is that it cannot be elaborated in the direction that past social theorists have often elaborated such hints. It cannot be turned into a more precise general theory of society. If we think of the 'tacit' part of a culture, or the 'normative system' of a society, as a body of individual habits which for the most part cannot be prevented from varying from one another, we cannot hope to do what past theorists have thought they could do with culture, normative systems and the like – treat them as collective objects with causal properties of the kind that we could hope to improve our knowledge of. But the point of what I have argued in this book is that the limitations of the inferences we may make about bodies of habit are profound. The character of the limitations bears directly on the question of what social theory can be. We deal with the habits we are trying to understand as through a fog. We have no access to them save by analogical reasoning, and no clear understanding of their inner causal structure because there is no collective causal object to understand.

114 The Opacity of Practice

To understand the implications of this way of thinking, it is useful to return to the history of social theory. The issue is this. If practices are no more than individual habits, with the properties of acquisition of individual habits, it seems that social theory, in its most ambitious forms, cannot live with them, for practice in this sense is not a determinate enough object to use in serious explanations. Yet the writings of social thinkers from Hobbes, with his 'manners maketh man', and Montesquieu to Parsons himself establish that social theory cannot live without the concept or one of its cognates, such as 'norms' which has the same debilities.

We may distinguish two general strategies in dealing with the problem of making inferences about practices in the tradition of social theory. One view, best exemplified in Weber, is to reason about unconscious aspects of action on more or less strict analogy to the conscious forms of the same things that are available to the individual. Thus the Protestant believer whose habits and emotional responses to pleasure and indulgence are formed in the inchoate emotional experiences of early childhood is to be understood in terms of the explicit doctrines of Calvin. For Weber, indeed, there is no real alternative to such an approach. Like rational choice theorists or economists who reason about 'revealed preferences', the revelation depends on an analogy between the preferences that the economic agent would articulate if he or she were able, or forced, to explain and justify his or her decisions explicitly. The limitations of this model are obvious: the whole range of habits that are not open to this kind of analogizing are lost. This is why Weber has next to nothing to say about the formation of *Weltanschauungen*: his way of approaching the domain of what I have called here mental habits assures that it is ideas and their consequences rather than the *weltanshauliche* conditions for ideas and their reception that occupy him. And he has no way of reasoning about unconscious consequences of experiences that do not have a conscious or explicit analogue. So this strategy is only a partial solution.

The second strategy is that of Durkheim and others, for whom the realm that Weber cannot have access to is important, but accessible through a certain kind of inference. For these thinkers, what we can observe in society, or even what is consciously thought by those of us in a society, is merely a manifestation of deeper causal structures or processes. Society is a great beast or machine of which the actions and thoughts of individuals are a part and product – as Tönnies poetically puts it, are 'surface messengers'. From these manifestations we may determine the structures and functions of, or induce the underlying principles of, this Leviathan. The hidden collective objects discussed in this book – be they norms or the *mentalités* of the ruling classes – are determinable from the manifestations. By inferring back from the manifestations we get to the real causal stuff itself.

The implication of what I have argued here for such a strategy of inference is this: if the 'real causal stuff', the existence of which is inferred, includes norms, practices, tacit rules and the like, and these things are understood as hidden collective objects, the causal story breaks down over transmission. We recognize the absurdities of Durkheim's own imagery. But the same kinds of problems hold for Bourdieu's idea of 'reproduction' or Parsons' notion of the introjection of norms. They are simply hidden under more contemporary metaphors. So these models, which seem to hold out such promise, are inherently flawed, at least if they are understood, as they are understood by those that have advanced them, as first approximations to more precise and determinate theoretical knowledge.

In each of these cases the project of inference starts well, with some new manifestation explained or some problem in previous attempts at inference resolved. But in time the process runs into the sand. Durkheim's effort to construct the laws of the *conscience collective*, for example, did not get beyond his apparent success in the explanation of suicide rates. The fatal attraction of these circular programmes of inference to an explanation derives from the fact that the programmes *have* 'successes'. It *is* possible to sustain various organic or mechanical analogies about society, and to 'make sense' of otherwise difficult-to-comprehend features of social life as 'manifestations' of inferred underlying processes. But these initial successes depend on a certain kind of inferential circularity. The explanatory facts are inferred to be so because they provide an explanation. The explanation is accepted as an explanation because it promises to be of more general bearing and significance than the thing explained, such as differences in suicide rates. But this promise is never properly kept. Moreover, there is a promise to the effect that these 'rough' explanations will be sharpened up, the concepts made more precise, and the predictions improved. And this promise is not kept either.

But the failure of the initially 'successful' inferences about the inner workings of the beast to produce much of additional value is usually not an especially clear-cut failure. In part this is because the original arguments were made in conjunction with programmatic statements that were unclear with respect to the future successes that would constitute validation for the programme. But the explanations still seem serviceable for the local settings in which they originated, and they often seem not only to account for the things they were devised to account for but also to illuminate new situations or contexts. As sociologists sometimes say, they are useful as 'sensitizing concepts', and indeed they come to have a role in many contexts in which precision and the trappings of science are not important simply by virtue of their utility in helping people get around in the face of their particular problems of action and comprehension. They go wrong where they are applied in inappropriate places and ways – which is the same as saying 'applied where they don't do any explanatory work or don't hold'. When they are raised to the level of generality of a totalizing theory of society or history, they claim universal applicability. But all totalizing social theories (other than purely formalistic theoretical constructions) so far have failed when they are applied outside the domain for which they were originally devised. This does not mean that there is a reason in principle why they had to fail. But the pattern gives rise to a very compelling induction.

The idea of 'practice' and its cognates has this odd kind of promissory utility. They promise that they can be turned into something more precise. But the value of the concepts is destroyed when they are pushed in the direction of meeting their promise.[3] New objects – *habitus* instead of norms, norms instead of *mores* – are proposed. New explanatory successes, usually restricted to a small range of phenomena, occur. The concepts of social theory have nine lives because the project has nine lives. Programme succeeds programme, and promise succeeds promise. So the project itself is never challenged, but it never succeeds either, at least in the way it would succeed if the structure of the beast were gradually being revealed. Instead we get, so to speak, different kinds of scans of the beast, each of which cannot be improved beyond a certain level of fuzziness, and each of which gives somewhat different and inconsistent or difficult-to-integrate pictures. Social theory is often written to solve the problem of integrating pictures – reconciling Marx and Durkheim or these two with George Herbert Mead and critical theory, or in earlier times Pareto, Marshall, Durkheim and Weber. Finding some sort of reductive standpoint which will render this task of integration superfluous is an alternative to these picture-integrating tasks.[4] And efforts to find such a reductive standpoint also follow one another with regularity – and fail regularly. The fatal charm of this perpetually half-successful enterprise is that, at first, the theories seem to work. But if what I have said here is correct, if there are no collective objects to be accounted for – causally, teleologically or structurally – but only individual habits, then there is nothing to sharpen up or make more precise. We are, so to speak, stuck at a particular level of fuzziness in our scans of the 'cultural' part of the great beast 'society'.

Concepts like 'tradition', however, have a life outside the project of constructing a general social theory. What, it may be wondered, are the implications of the argument of the book for these uses. For some uses, the difference doesn't matter at all. The use of the term 'practices' in a descriptive way in historical writing to designate patterns of behaviour that seem to us to be similar and may be said to have been passed along among persons who lived together seems like an innocuous use. It fits with the notion that the transmission may be only through the performances and observances of the common life. But historical claims about privileged forms of transmission often are turned to other uses. The argument of the nineteenth century, to the effect that no ethnic group that had not possessed such traditions as the moot for a millennium could hope to sustain a democracy, is a case in point. It fails because the model of transmission as multi-generation marination is ludicrous. In the case of artificial intelligence models of tacit knowledge, the implications are simple: the possibility must be accepted that there is no particular connection between (a) the assumptions one builds into a model that emulates some particular domain of reasoning and (b) some sort of body of assumptions that are supposedly shared in the community of persons who reason in a fashion that can be emulated by an artificial intelligence model.

In the case of politics, the implications are these. If traditions are not object-like things, they cannot be 'preserved' or for that matter 'rooted out'. What can be changed are observances and the experiences people have that produce the habits that they bring to politics. We may provide experiences in terms of which people learn new political habits.

It would be, on this account, impossible to bemoan the supposed fact that modern people lack a tradition, as MacIntyre does, or claim that the British have a political tradition and the Americans, Germans or some other group do not.[5] What these claims might mean instead is that there are no effective public observances, rituals or memorializing acts, or not enough in the way of political proficiency-demanding performances, to produce enough in the way of habit to enable people in these other political systems to act in concert without constantly appealing to the explicit rule book. But stated in this different way the claim is much less compelling, and more obviously untrue in some of the cases to which it is applied. It also points, at least, to a cure for the problem of an inadequate tradition or to means by which a tradition in this new sense can be preserved or changed. But the remedies, the observance of public rituals or the promotion of political learning experiences, turn out to be things we already do and that ordinary people, if not intellectuals, do suppose have some effects of the right kind.

Practice relativism

Relativism, the kind of relativism that is held to derive from the practice-relative character of truth, presents more daunting problems. Radical cultural differences, after all, are pervasive facts well recognized by enlightened people – only the Victorians had the temerity to regard the rest of the world as languishing in error and superstition. Here, as in earlier discussions, it is perhaps useful to scrutinize the facts. In the middle of the nineteenth century probability thinkers had an emblematic (and as it happens apparently false) story that the proportion of dead letters at the Paris post office never varied from year to year. The inexorably stable workings of probability were supposed to account for this fact. As I suggested in the last chapter, Evans-Pritchard's ethnographic report on the Azande and their supposed lack of theoretical interest in the contradictory implications of their use of poison oracles is more than a bit like this story. It is too good to be true, or too congenial to the interpretations placed upon it for the facts to be so simple. But in this case it appears that we have all the facts we need – they are ethnographic facts about a collectively shared way of thinking that is radically alien. And because we have no alternative, we must accept the hypothesis that the fundamental presuppositions of the Azande differ from ours.

The kinds of explanations we apply to our neighbours and colleagues are very different from those that we might apply to the beliefs of the Azande. To explain the difference between, for example, one individual's faith in God and another's disbelief in the existence of God, it would suffice to point to such banalities as the fact that there is no way to settle the question of the existence of God by reference to what are usually regarded as facts. One may add to this an explanation: that a person may have a need to believe that results from some sort of special circumstance, such as the fact that the belief is comforting, or that the person was raised in an environment in which religious belief was important and religious observance central.

Are these cases of 'relativism' or are they merely cases of intelligible disagreement which are neither errors nor the products of commitment to different systems? It could be, for example, that our believer and disbeliever do *not* agree that the facts do not enable one to decide the question of the existence of God, and therefore agree that they disagree as to what constitutes a fact. But is this a disagreement that results from 'commitment' to 'different systems'? Or is it, too, a kind of ordinary personal disagreement?

To raise the question of what might be a proper example of 'relativism' is to open a Pandora's box: it is difficult to find a clear formulation of the 'problem of relativism' in the first place, and there probably is no one 'problem'. But one hypothesis might be the following: the problem of relativism which looms so large today in academic discourse, and provides an interpretation for what seems to be a world full of intractable intellectual conflicts over morals and ultimate truth, or a world full of multiple interpretations each of which is equally valid, is a by-product of the use of the analogies that have been discussed in this book.

The idea of intractable conflicts resulting from different fundamental premises, or different fundamental commitments, depends on the analogy between ordinary belief and action and belief and action within explicit theories. The language of 'commitment' that runs through this literature also depends on this analogy. We are depicted as being committed to premises – tacit premises. Learning something in the ways we ordinarily learn and becoming convinced by it – a causal process – is reconstrued in terms of an analogy with theoretical reasoning from premises. The analogical construal proceeds by reasoning backwards from present beliefs to hypothesized premises. The 'most basic' of these premises cannot, by definition, be justified. They therefore have to be 'accepted' in another way. Analogies supply this need: an analogical act of 'commitment' explains the analogical 'acceptance' of the analogically posited 'premiss'.

The case of the Azande is so compelling, I suggested, because we are *de facto* prevented from treating this case as we would treat a neighbour or colleague who dabbled in mysticism or believed in luck. With neighbours and colleagues, we might be puzzled, but we would explain their beliefs, to the extent that we wanted to, on the grounds of their individual peculiarities – facts of biography, personality, circumstance and the like. If we discovered that our neighbours engaged in occult practices, we would revise our understanding of them as persons. The idea that they are sealed within some sort of closed system of assumptions which prevents them from grasping the error of their ways would never arise. But our vast resources for accounting for individual peculiarities are simply useless to us in the case of the Azande. We could not apply our usual explanations of disagreement. We are forced to construe their sayings and doings 'relativistically'. We have no alternative. We do not have any information that would have allowed us to construct any other explanation, and it appears that there can be no such information.

But we are also prevented from accounting for the case as an ordinary disagreement *de jure*. Terms in the family of presupposition, tacit premiss and the like disable our ordinary ways of accounting for disagreements systematically. Our usual vocabulary for accounting for differences – different experiences, different backgrounds, different but intelligible belief-choices in the face of inconclusive evidence, and so on – simply does not apply to 'tacit premisses'. The reasons for this are simple. The usual means of accounting are causal. They point to different experiences, different properties of persons, different backgrounds and the like. The language of 'tacit premisses' is analogical. The explanations of these purely notional objects are also analogical. People are 'committed' to presuppositions, 'share' them and so forth. The analogies are to ordinary public acts of affirmation, consent and the like. There is a radical failure to mesh between these analogical explanations operating in a notional world and the commonplace considerations we apply to disagreements.

Accepting the idea of fundamental, rationally irreconcilable differences in tacit premisses – relativism – seems to be a solution. The failure of commonplace considerations to account for certain kinds of disagreement becomes a *ground* for accepting the 'tacit premiss' picture. And there is another powerful ground: the picture seems to work so well – to be of instrumental value – in contexts that are important to us. We can come to understand other people by taking them to be reasoning from different premisses. We can come to mutual understandings of our differences with other people by coming to agreements over what is in dispute, and in this kind of negotiation of the issues in dispute it is often useful for communication and for self-understanding to identify and make explicit premisses which those with whom one is disagreeing or wishes to understand do not.

It should be noted, however, that these successes are wholly instrumental. They do not necessarily point to a new factual domain of premisses that are 'in the mind' or practices that are 'inscribed on the body'. Consider a remark made by Richard Rorty, 'that each philosophical generation points out some unconscious presuppositions built into the vocabulary of its predecessors'.[6] We can take this as a metaphorical locational claim – that 'unconscious presuppositions' are hidden, so to speak, in the woodwork of language or indeed are part of the woodwork of language. Or we can take the point entirely in an instrumental way, and construe these 'unconscious presuppositions' as a formulation of what we would have to believe in order to reason explicitly as past generations do with the words they use.

The approach I have taken in this book would suggest that the locational version of the claim is misguided: the presuppositions are not 'built into' language, except in the sense that the person who masters the explicit reasoning formulated in the language in question must acquire different habits in order to master the reasoning and language in the first place.[7] Suppose there are no non-public collective facts of language that others, such as past philosophers, shared and we do not, much less common items buried in their unconscious that are not found in ours. This leads to a different picture, in which the only 'system' or theory to be found is that which is explicitly stated, and that the only relevant knowledge, skills or habits that are 'tacit' are the habits one needs in order to master explicit theories, performances and the like, and these may vary from person to person.

Stanley Cavell's famous comment that we learn language and the world together may be revised to fit this new picture. Not only do we learn language and the world together, at the same time as we learn them we acquire habits that enable us to be more or less proficient in using both language and the world. To learn and comprehend is to acquire habits, habits that enable one to go on. And this does not happen only in 'magic moments', but continuously – even in the course of reading through and understanding a text.[8] But there is no reason to think these habits are shared. There is no need to suppose that there are *common* tacit parts of our 'theory of the world' or 'cultural system', and there is no need to suppose that there is any sort of common object like a common 'theory of the world' or 'cultural system' at all.

If we accept this picture, a great deal may be conceded with respect to the *instrumental* utility or convenience of the 'mind full of presuppositions' model. In the history of science, in the history of political ideas, and in other places where similar terms are used in different ways, it is useful to think of these differences as involving different premises. But this utility misleads us, if we think that we are identifying psychologically real bases of the thought of other people.

The difficulty is this. Ordinarily we account for disagreements in terms of error. If we encounter a difference of opinion in which no error has been made, we consider the difference to be intelligible and unproblematic. We do not regard theists as having committed an error by believing in God, or atheists as committing an error by disbelieving. We accept that there is no procedure or relevant evidence that can settle such questions. Indeed, many other differences of opinion we put down to taste, past experience and so forth. To be sure, the parties to a given dispute can claim that the disagreements are not merely intelligible disagreements in the face of procedures and evidence that are incapable of settling the disagreements, but rather disagreements over the validity of the procedures and the meaning of the evidence. But at this meta-level we have the same option. These disagreements are also open to treatment as ordinary differences of opinion, differences in the face of insufficient grounds for settling them. To be sure, they are more difficult to treat in this way, because the 'procedures' in dispute are notional. We cannot say they were acquired erroneously, as we can for ordinary information, because we cannot say how they were acquired at all.

Our only choice, it appears, is to treat them as 'givens', and accept that different people have different givens. But this is our choice only if we think there are such things as givens. If we do not, we can simply treat them as disagreements that we have no way of resolving. The former has 'relativistic' implications in the practice-relativistic sense discussed here; the latter does not. The practice relativist must interpret at least some disagreements, over 'fundamental' premises, as immune to resolution through new experiences. The argument of this book is that there is no reason to think there are such fundamental premises, or that the causal stuff which the idea of 'fundamental premises' is supposed to correspond to is immune to new experiences or to becoming supplanted by new habits.

The argument of this book has led in a different direction. It suggests that the causal side of coming to belief and understanding and the justificatory side diverge: that coming to belief and to understanding involves the acquisition of habits, and that these acquisitions need not be thought of as acquisitions of a common object, and consequently the kinds of analogical reasoning we employ when we construe the explicit beliefs, actions and observances of others as following from different tacit premises should be understood in a wholly instrumental way. There is no epistemic moral to be drawn from the fact that the analogical process of tracing disputes back to supposed hidden premises may lead back to premises that are in conflict. The conflicts are themselves notional.

In Chapter 1, I pointed out that practices have come to serve as a naturalistic substitute for foundations or first principles, as a kind of backstop or terminus in the chain of justification that we accept as a terminus because it is not itself a justification, but a fact in the causal world. The point of this substitution is that practice is opaque. There are no justifications lurking behind practice, only the murky world, it is supposed, of social determination in which practices are embedded and which sustains them. This imagery leaves us with the same problems of relativism and irrationality that we were left with in the case of the unjustifiable basic presuppositions of paradigms, and with the same imagery of horizons and imprisonment. But those who employ this imagery wish to have their cake and eat it too. They wish to have a causal notion, because only a causal notion can be an endpoint, a 'basis', and they wish for it to be a premiss-like thing, because only if people do not share basic premisses is there relativistic disagreement. My point is that practices cannot be both causal and shared: when we tried to conceive of them as both causal and shared we failed.

The romantic picture of the intellect immured should be left to the cultural historians of the future as a curiosity. The only prison here, the only opacity, is the Maussian one: we cannot do anything to get behind the notion of practice, either in a causal or a justificatory way, because practices are not objects, but are rather explanatory constructions that solve specific problems of comparison and unmet expectations. The Maussian analyst must formulate discoveries for an audience which has similar expectations. But breaches in expectations occur adventitiously, and reveal no more than specific, limited differences. We cannot identify practices as such. We cannot even separate the 'social' part of practice from the natural part. The same holds for artificial intelligence emulations of human thought and conduct. Success and failure occur only within preset problem domains, specific sets of tasks which are to be emulated.[9]

The picture that I have developed here is one in which practices is a word not for some sort of mysterious hidden collective object, but for the individual formations of habit that are the condition for the performances and emulations that make up life. No one is immured by these habits. They are, rather, the stepping-stones we use to get from one bit of mastery to another.

Notes

Chapter 1 Practices and their Conceptual Kin

1 Ludwig Wittgenstein, *On Certainty*, ed. G.E.M. Anscombe and G.H. von Wright, transl. Denis Paul and G.E.M. Anscombe (J. & J. Harper, New York, 1969), p. 15e.
2 Hubert Dreyfus, 'The mind in Husserl: intentionality in the fog', *Times Literary Supplement*, 12 July 1991, p. 25.
3 David Bell, *Husserl* (Routledge, London, 1990), p. 229. Bell notes a similarity to Husserl's view that, as Bell states it, 'The identity and the integrity of a society or culture, according to Husserl, are functions of the possession by its members of a body of beliefs and practices "taken for granted" and "made use of as unquestioned and available"' (Ibid.). The quotations are from Edmund Husserl, *The Crisis of the European Sciences and Transcendental Phenomenology* (Northwestern University Press, Evanston, IL, 1970), transl. D. Carr, p. 112. Bell calls the stuff 'possessed' by the members of a society 'inherited commitments'. This language, and the theses it is used to express, is my subject in this book.
4 Hubert L. Dreyfus, *Being-in-the-World: A Commentary on Heidegger's Being and Time, Division I* (MIT Press, Cambridge, MA, 1991), p. 17. Cf. Pierre Bourdieu, *Outline of a Theory of Practice*, transl. Richard Nice (Cambridge at the University Press, 1977).
5 Sherry Ortner, 'Theory in anthropology since the sixties', *Comparative Studies in Society and History*, 16 (1984), pp. 126–66.
6 Michael Oakeshott, *Rationalism in Politics and Other Essays* (Methuen,

London, 1962); Michael Polanyi, *Personal Knowledge* (University of Chicago Press, Chicago, 1958), Gilbert Ryle, 'Knowing how and knowing that', *Proceedings of the Aristotelian Society*, XLVI (1945–6), pp. 1–16; Alasdair MacIntyre, *After Virtue* (University of Notre Dame Press, Notre Dame, IN, 1981); H.-G. Gadamer, *Truth and Method* (Seabury, New York, 1975); Richard Rorty, *Contingency, Irony, and Solidarity* (Cambridge at the University Press, 1989); W.V.O. Quine and Jon Elster, *The Cement of Society* (Cambridge at the University Press, 1989), p. 106, cf. pp. 104–5; David Lewis, *Convention* (Harvard University Press, Cambridge, MA, 1969); Roberto Mangabeira Unger, *False Necessity* (Cambridge at the University Press, 1987), p. 96. An excellent introduction to many of these concepts may be found in J.C. Nyíri and Barry Smith, eds, *Practical Knowledge: Outlines of a Theory of Tradition and Skills* (Croom Helm, London, 1988).

7 Ferdinand Tönnies, *Custom: An Essay on Social Codes* (Free Press, New York, 1961), transl. A. Borenstein. The German title of this book was *Die Sitte*.

8 A historical treatment of the concept of *Sitte* may be found in Werner Woschnak, *Zum Begriff der Sitte* (Verlag der Österreichischen Akademie der Wissenschaften, Vienna, 1988). This study stresses various conceptual oppositions: between *Sitte* and power, *Sitte* and law, *Sitte* and life, and so forth.

9 In the 1710 edition of *A Treatise Concerning the Principles of Human Knowledge* he remarks parenthetically that 'two ways there are of learning a language, either by rule or by practice'. This suggests that the two are equivalent. In a later version of the same passage Berkeley changes his mind and says, 'It is very possible to *write* improperly *through too strict an observance of general grammar rules.*' The changed text captures the ambivalence that is one basis for the notion of practice as a surplus – the difference between proper writing and writing over-governed by rules (see sect. cviii).

10 David Hume, *Enquiries Concerning the Human Understanding and Concerning the Principles of Morals*, ed. L.A. Selby-Bigge, 2nd edn (Clarendon Press, Oxford, 1902), p. 39.

11 Ibid., p. 43. 'By employing that word [custom], we pretend not to have given the ultimate reason of such a propensity. We only point out a principle of human nature, which is universally acknowledged, and which is well known by its effects.' In contrast to an 'ultimate reason', a custom is only 'ultimate' in the *de facto* sense (ibid.).

12 Kant's discussion loaded the dice in favour of the answer he preferred. He commented that 'not every activity can be called a 'practice' and suggested that 'a practice' be *defined* as an activity seeking a goal 'which is conceived as a result of following certain general principles of procedure'. He could then concede that 'a link and transition is needed between theory' (meaning the general principles) and practice, but conclude that the link was no more than the 'act of judgment' by which the practitioner decides that something has

fallen under a rule (I. Kant, 'Theory and practice concerning the common saying: This may be true in theory but does not apply to practice', in *The Philosophy of Kant*, ed. Carl J. Friedrich [Modern Library, New York, 1949], p. 412).

13 Computer modelling of cognitive capacities is fraught with philosophical complexities. It will suffice here to observe that even the most fundamental notions, such as information and representation, trade on ambiguities between their status in the language of interpretation and their use as causal terms for machine processes in computers. So the language of artificial intelligence and cognitive science provides no escape from the problems of causality.

Chapter 2 Practices as Causes

1 John Austin, *A Plea for the Constitution* (J. Murray, London, 1859), p. 16.
2 Ibid., p. 7.
3 Charles Camic, 'The matter of habit', *American Journal of Sociology*, 91 (1986), pp. 1039-87.
4 John Dewey, *Human Nature and Conduct* (Modern Library, New York, 1922).
5 John Austin, *The Province of Jurisprudence Determined and the Uses of the Study of Jurisprudence* (Weidenfeld & Nicolson, London, 1954), p. 37.
6 Ibid., pp. 50-1.
7 Ibid., pp. 51-2.
8 There are obvious analogies in ordinary life to habits being trimmed to look the same. Tutoring and disciplining are intentional means by which people are induced to respond habitually in ways that are the same, or sufficiently similar for them to act in concert. 'Wild' or untutored habituation may have similar effects to tutored habituation. So it is tempting to run the two kinds of habituation together, and to treat untutored habituation as a kind of disciplinary process with no disciplinarian or teacher. Foucault reasons in this way. Disciplining, however, is an intentional process, with a purpose. So it becomes meaningful to ask what purpose lies behind the disciplining that occurs where there is no disciplinarian, and to ask who benefits from the process of disciplinary 'trimming to look the same' in society.
9 Austin, *Plea*, p. 41.
10 Marcel Mauss, 'Body techniques', in *Sociology and Psychology: Essays by Marcel Mauss* (Routledge & Kegan Paul, London, 1979), pp. 97-135.
11 Ibid., p. 100.
12 Cf. M. Gopnik, 'Feature-blind grammar and dysphasia', *Nature*, 334 (1990), p. 715.

13 William Graham Sumner, *Folkways* (Ginn, Boston, 1907), p. 79.
14 Ibid.
15 This approach is undermined by the impossibility of getting people into a situation of collective decision-making who do not already share some sort of common *mores* – such as the practice of promising and keeping promises.
16 Cf. Max Weber, *Critique of Stammler* (Free Press, New York, 1975), pp. 166–7.
17 Friedrich Nietzsche, *Daybreak* (Cambridge at the University Press, 1982), aph. 9.

Chapter 3 Practices as Presuppositions

1 Ludwig Wittgenstein, *Tractatus Logico-Philosophicus* (Routledge & Kegan Paul, London, 1961), sect. 4.002. This presumably is among the views he abandoned in favour of the notion of *Lebensformen* which is discussed in more detail in Chapter 5.
2 A long post-Kantian tradition thought that there was a way around this problem. Kant's idea was that there is some sort of ultimate answer to the question 'What must we presuppose?' and his philosophical project depended on the notion that there is at least a small set of ultimate presuppositions which are universal and necessary for experience. These presuppositions, had they existed, would have been attributable as psychological possessions of people by inference from the fact that they experience the world. Presuppositions that are not universally necessary of course cannot be understood in this way.
3 People are notoriously inaccurate in reporting on their own mental processes and there is no reason to think reports on presuppositions are different.
4 Patrick Gardiner, 'Jakob Burckhardt', *Encyclopedia of Philosophy*, I, p. 427 (Macmillan and Free Press, New York, 1967).
5 Steve Woolgar, 'Some remarks about positionism: a reply to Collins and Yearley', in Andrew Pickering, ed., *Science as Practice and Culture* (University of Chicago Press, Chicago, 1992), pp. 327–42. See also Steve Woolgar, *Science: The Very Idea* (Tavistock, New York, 1988).
6 Harvey Sacks, 'On the analyzability of stories by children', in John J. Gumperz and Dell Hymes, eds, *Directions in Sociolinguistics: The Enthnography of Communication* (Holt, Rinehart & Winston, New York, 1972), p. 329.
7 Ibid.
8 I am indebted to Mike Lynch for this formulation.
9 Descriptions of this object which explains order vary. Garfinkel and Wieder speak of 'locally produced, naturally accountable phenomena of order, logic,

reason, meaning, method, and so on, in and as of the unavoidable and irremediable haecceity of immortal, ordinary society' (Harold Garfinkel and D. Lawrence Wieder, 'Two incommensurable, asymmetrically alternate technologies of social analysis', in Graham Watson and Lauren Seiler, eds, *Text in Context: Contributions to Ethnomethodology* [Sage, Newbury Park, CA, 1992], p. 175). The explanation, in this case signalled by the term 'production', is built into the description. Hilbert is a bit clearer: 'Ethnomethods are social practices whereby members orient to a presupposed social-structural order, reifying and reproducing it in the course of their activity and *imposing its reality on each other as they go*' (Richard Hilbert, *The Classical Roots of Ethnomethodology: Durkheim, Weber and Garfinkel* [University of North Carolina Press, Chapel Hill, 1992], p. 194). But this leaves open the question of where they are located. Hilbert says they are not 'owned' by anyone, but 'social at the outset'. Presumably by 'not owned' he means they are not possessed exclusively, otherwise they could not be learnable and teachable, for this implies individual 'possession'. The term 'embedded' leads to the same problem. If the thing doing the explaining, the practice, is embedded in the routines, how does it get out so that it can be learned by persons? The full implications of this question will become clear in the next chapter.

Chapter 4 Transmission

1 Friedrich Nietzsche, *Daybreak* (Cambridge at the University Press, 1982), aph. 34.
2 The literary criticism literature, it must be said, is rife with such substitutes, used in conjunction with the notion of 'practices' or on their own, or in various combinations with one another. The two kinds that are instantly recognizable from the point of view of social theory are the appeal to 'power', 'interest' (as in class interest) and the like, as though these were unproblematic substantive notions, and the appeal to philosophical anthropologies, such as the claim that people are inherently driven to 'struggle to avoid...fictiveness' (Morse Peckham, *Explanation and Power* [Seabury, New York, 1979], p. 100). Of course it is the general failure of these theories as backstops that motivated the appeal to 'practices' described in Chapter 1. In the final chapter, I give some reasons for supposing that a return to these forms of theorizing is misguided.
3 I leave aside for the moment the question of whether Wittgenstein himself wished to argue in this way.
4 Hans Reichenbach, *The Rise of Scientific Philosophy* (University of

California Press, Berkeley and Los Angeles, 1951), p. 285. The text is a parallel to Tönnies, especially in its discussion of the authority of parents. In his discussion of group ethics and their 'conglomeration' he resembles Durkheim (cf. pp. 286–7).
5 Ibid.
6 Moreover, the more mechanistic or computer-like our image of the mind becomes, the less room there is for these mysterious collective forces – in a world without intention, there is no place for collective intentions either.
7 Stanley Fish, *Doing What Comes Naturally* (Duke University Press, Durham, NC, 1989), p. 153.
8 Ibid., p. 33.
9 Ibid., pp. 30–1.
10 Ibid., pp. 30–2.
11 Ibid., p. 150.
12 Ibid., p. 153.
13 Emile Durkheim, *The Rules of Sociology Method*, W.D. Halls, transl. (Free Press, New York, 1982), pp. 121–3.
14 The code is, so to speak, composed of practices, or as Fish puts it, 'the code ... is inseparable from the practices it enables (it cannot be reduced to a formal rule)' (Fish, *Doing*, p. 151), but the locus of purpose and change is in the code in the sense of a kind of collective object with purposes, an enterprise. Single practices, presumably, are not enterprises, do not have purposes, and do not elaborate themselves in the same manner. Fish's source in this discussion is a work by the ethnomethodologist D. Lawrence Weider, *Language and Social Reality: The Case of Telling the Convict Code* (Mouton, The Hague, 1974).
15 Fish quotes Weider's own remark to the effect that the code is 'self and setting elaborative' (Fish, *Doing*, p. 150).
16 Ibid., p. 151.
17 Mark Poster, 'Sexuality and discourse: a response to Roy Porter on Foucault', *Contention*, 1 (1991), p. 85.
18 We have already seen some utilitarian examples, and the case of Hume, whose use of the terms habit and custom are more or less interchangeable.
19 The salience of this problem in literary theory is shown in the inadequacies of attempts to paper over the issue. Fish points out that the reception theorist Wolfgang Iser vacillates on this issue. On the one hand, 'Iser never gives any examples of readers going their own way ... because the reader he can imagine is always the creature of the machine he has already set in motion; in every analysis the reader is described as being "guided," "controlled," "induced," and even "jerked," ... and what he is being guided or jerked by are textual elements that are themselves the product of interpretation' (Fish, *Doing*, p. 84). At the same time Iser himself criticizes what he describes as theories 'which give the impression that texts automatically imprint themselves on the reader's mind' (quoted in ibid., p. 85). Fish comments that 'his

theory cannot get off the ground unless it claims exactly that for the set of directions that guide the reader's "meaning assembly" ', i.e., the process by which the reader constructs his reception of a text.
20 This idea has a wide appeal. Jeffrey Alexander writes that 'discourses ... not only communicate information, structuring reality in a cognitive or expressive way: they ... also perform a forceful, evaluative task' (Jeffrey C. Alexander and Philip Smith, 'The discourse of American civil society: a new proposal for cultural studies', *Theory and Society*, forthcoming).
21 Aryeh Botwinich, *Participation and Tacit Knowledge in Plato, Machiavelli and Hobbes* (University Press of America, Lanham, MD, 1986).
22 Iser, quoted in Fish, *Doing*, pp. 79, 85.
23 Freud reconceptualizes Le Bon in terms of the introjection of super-ego elements – the crowd for him too is a situation of regression to the plasticity and openness to introjection of early childhood (Sigmund Freud, *Group Psychology and the Analysis of the Ego* [Norton, New York, 1959], p. 49).
24 This example is also discussed by Spranger, to whom we turn shortly.
25 H.M. Collins, *Artificial Experts: Social Knowledge and Intelligent Machines* (MIT Press, Cambridge, MA, 1990), pp. 94–5.
26 Eduard Spranger, *Types of Men: The Psychology and Ethics of Personality* (Max Niemeyer Verlag, Halle, 1928), authorized translation of the fifth German edition, p. viii.
27 Ibid., p. 372.
28 Ibid., p. 56.
29 In this respect and others, the argument resembles Michael Oakeshott's 1933 *Experience and its Modes* (Cambridge at the University Press, 1971). One similarity is crucial. In modern societies, the attitudes or 'modes' (social, political, theoretical, religious and aesthetic) *are* the different 'forms of life'. The law, for example, is not such a form, because the purpose of the law is to be found in values revealed by other orientations.
30 Spranger, *Types*, p. 110.
31 Among other things, it includes 'objective' values, which we may or may not have access to, just as we may be unable to understand the saying of Christ quoted by Spranger. This, it may be noted, is consistent with Wittgenstein's own remarks on values. Cf. Ludwig Wittgenstein, *Culture and Value*, transl. Peter Winch (University of Chicago Press, Chicago, 1980).
32 Saul A. Kripke, *Wittgenstein: On Rules and Private Language*, (Harvard University Press, Cambridge, MA, 1982), pp. 90–1.
33 Ibid., p. 91.
34 Of course, the tests allow a certain amount of error. The putative adder 'will be judged by the community to have (mastered the concept) if his particular responses agree with those of the community in enough cases, especially the simple ones (and if his "wrong" answers are not often *bizarrely* wrong, as in "5" for "68+57", but seem to agree with ours in *procedure*, even when he makes a "computational mistake")' (ibid., p. 92).

35 Ibid., p. 92.
36 Ibid., p. 95.
37 Ibid., p. 96.
38 Ibid., p. 69.
39 Ibid., p. 97.
40 Perhaps it should be added that these doubts are not trivial, and that one can go seriously wrong in understanding the everyday world. This at least is the basis of 'cognitive therapy', which treats personality disorders as the product of schemes, beliefs and rules that produce 'thinking, affect, and behavior' that is self-defeating but self-perpetrating because it 'has been functional for the patient across many life situations (A.T. Beck, A.F. Freeman and Associates, *Cognitive Therapy of Personality Disorders* [Guilford, New York, 1990], p. 7).
41 This lapse into sociological jargon should by now be expected. In this case it signals that Kripke's social theory is different from the more complex one from which Wittgenstein borrowed *Lebensformen*.

Chapter 5 Change and History

1 David Hackett Fischer, *Albion's Seed: Four British Folkways in America* (Oxford University Press, New York, 1989).
2 Paul Hoch, 'Institutional intellectual migrations in the nucleation of new scientific specialties', *Studies in the History and Philosophy of Science*, 18 (1987), pp. 481–500.
3 Alan Macfarlane, *The Origins of English Individualism* (Cambridge University Press, New York, 1979), p. 170.
4 Eric Hobsbawm and Terence Ranger, eds, *The Invention of Tradition* (Cambridge University Press, New York, 1983).
5 Alasdair MacIntyre, *Whose Justice, Which Rationality?* (University of Notre Dame Press, Notre Dame, IN, 1988). A similar notion arises in the writings of Hans-Georg Gadamer, whose term is 'the fusion of horizons' (Hans-Georg Gadamer, *Truth and Method* [Seabury, New York, 1975], p. 273).
6 Max Weber, 'Objectivity in social science and social policy', in *Methodology of the Social Sciences* (Free Press, New York, 1949), p. 112. 'Unreflectively utilized viewpoints' is an image consistent with the model of habitualized ideology. But it is less clear that the new light in question is always the result of explicit ideology.

The root of the difficulty is that the Weberian tool kit for addressing cultural change is somewhat limited. He can deal with the fate of bearers of ideas, with charisma, and with rationalization. But only charisma is a source of cultural novelty: one of the powers attributed to charismatic leaders is the power of creating new values. But these new values are themselves presumably explicit values or perhaps exemplary persons who are treated as

explicit models to follow. The concept of rationalization presumably also proceeds on the explicit, conscious level as well. If these tools are not sufficient to account for the cultural light 'moving on', there is a gap between the sociology and the methodology.
7 Stanley Fish, *Doing What Comes Naturally* (Duke University Press, Durham, NC, 1989), p. 143.
8 Ibid., pp. 143-4.
9 Ibid., p. 144.
10 Ibid., p. 146.
11 Ibid., p. 147.
12 Ibid., p. 149.
13 Ibid., p. 98.
14 Oddly enough, he quotes a textbook pronouncement of yet another sociologist, Robert Nisbet, on the topic of the identity of objects which change (Fish, *Doing*, pp. 152-3). Fish's solution to the problem of change is similar to that of Pitirim Sorokin, who 'solved' the problem by declaring social change to be 'immanent'.
15 Ibid., p. 152.
16 Ibid., p. 153. How something homogeneous like the collective purposes he describes are open to change *by* practices or the products of practice is never made clear. A pragmatist answer to this question would be that failures of the project on the project's own terms can produce changes in goals. But this kind of change would require innovation in goals. Scrapping goals is always conceivable. But inventing new goals is no easier to reconcile with the notion of closure than is any other innovation.
17 Fish embraces the notion that practices are partly or even largely tacit (e.g. in *Doing*, pp. 32, 44-5), and does give an account of imparting skills and acquiring them through mastering activities, contrasting this to learning and applying rules (*Doing*, p. 124) - i.e., the Kantian 'theory plus judgment' model. This account does not explain how the same practices get imparted, or even try to do so.
18 Clifford Geertz, *Local Knowledge: Further Essays in Interpretative Anthropology* (Basic Books, New York, 1983), p. 84.
19 E.E. Evans-Pritchard, *Witchcraft, Oracles, and Magic among the Azande*, abridged edn. (Clarendon Press, Oxford, 1976, originally published 1937).
20 'The sorcerer and his magic', *Structural Anthropology* (Doubleday Anchor, New York, 1967), p. 161. He is unable to produce examples of such cases, curiously enough. He substantiates his argument to the effect that magic is essentially 'intellectual' and 'a new system of reference' (p. 178) by showing how various failures of magic are accounted for within the intellectual scheme of magical thought.
21 Mircea Eliade, *The Sacred and the Profane* (Harcourt, New York, 1959), p. 33. The story is misrepresented by Eliade as fact. His source presents it as folklore, and describes quite different events. Cf. B. Spencer and F.J. Gillen,

The Arunta: A Study of a Stone Age People (Macmillan, London, 1927), p. 388.

22 Major uses of the case by philosophers include Michael Polanyi's in *Personal Knowledge: Towards a Post-Critical Philosophy* (University of Chicago Press, Chicago, 1958), pp. 287–8, in which the Azande are compared to Freudians and Marxists, and Peter Winch's 'Understanding a primitive Society', *American Philosophical Quarterly*, 1 (1964), pp. 307–24, in which Evans-Pritchard is criticized for pushing Zande thought to conclusions it would not naturally reach. Both are celebrations of 'closure'.

23 However dubious Kripke's picture of the creation of rules by primal 'agreement' may be as a general account of the acquisition of rules, it presents a plausible picture of one kind of case of rule-learning, and there is no reason to suppose that this kind of rule learning is excluded in the cases described by Fish or Lévi-Strauss. We do not need to suppose that a 'way of thinking' or a 'rule' is, however, a collective entity. All we need to suppose is that someone can be taught or trained to reason in a different way that reaches similar conclusions.

24 This will be dealt with in Chapter 6.

25 Kripke, presumably, would collapse the two notions, and this is one reason why Kripke's Wittgenstein is implausible as social theory: however credible the model of rule-creation through primal agreement is in particular cases, it is incredible as an account of culture or 'forms of life' as a whole. The acquisition of a culture, or an 'inherited background', cannot be imagined to consist of a series of separable and equally primal acts of agreement. As Wittgenstein, following Spranger, seems to suggest, something like a form of life seems instead to be a condition for the acquisition of knowledge or for communication, such as the communication or understanding of the Christian message, in Spranger's example.

26 T.S. Eliot, 'Notes toward a definition of culture', in *Christianity and Culture* (Harcourt Brace Jovanovich, New York, 1968), p. 104.

27 *Rationalism in Politics and Other Essays* (Methuen, London, 1962), p. 48. Oakeshott's classic statement on the question of what a tradition is may be found on pp. 128–9.

28 In one passage Oakeshott describes the Germans as 'the only European people which did start more or less with a blank sheet and became philosophers before they had learned how to live' ('The Universities'), in Timothy Fuller, ed., *The Voice of Liberal Learning: Michael Oakeshott on Education* (New Haven, CT, Yale University Press, 1989), p. 119.

Chapter 6 The Opacity of Practice

1 Anne von der Lieth Gardner, *An Artificial Intelligence Approach to Legal Reasoning* (MIT Press, Cambridge, MA, 1987).

2 Barry Barnes, *The Nature of Power* (University of Illinois Press, Urbana, 1988); Roberto Mangabiera Unger, *False Necessity* (Cambridge University Press, Cambridge, 1987), pp. 41–55.
3 The grand social theory of the nineteenth century and the first half of the twentieth was largely teleological and causal, and more teleological than causal. In the course of the twentieth century there has been a transition to programmes in which meaning, structures of meaning, semiotic significance and the like have taken on explanatory autonomy. They have themselves come to be explanations, final terms, in the analysis of the phenomena of mass media, literature and so forth. In part this is simply a reflection of the logic of the notion of 'shared presuppositions' with which programmes such as Mannheim's sociology of knowledge or Alfred Schütz and Merleau-Ponty's social phenomenology begin. But presuppositions, as we saw in Chapter 3, are a kind of explanatory dead end, unless one can explain how they are acquired and change. Marxism provided at least the illusion that some kind of explanation of this sort existed, and could be extracted from the teleological historical picture constructed by Marx.

The intellectual life both of Marxism and the notion of presupposition, especially in the sense of ideology, was extended by this alliance, and by the quasi-explanatory devices invented to account for the links between ideological 'superstructures' and the unchallenged 'facts' of the needs of ideological legitimation and hegemony of 'bourgeois society', patriarchal domination, European colonialism or American racism and imperialism – though the explanatory force of these 'facts' obviously depends on the validity of some historical picture of social theory in which they are themselves given some sort of causal or teleological significance, and these pictures are subject to the same sorts of limitations discussed above. If we ignore these considerations, and treat the interpretive schemes of feminism, literary Marxism and the like as explanations of the significance of the specific texts and text-like things that are objects of interpretation, the same pattern appears. There is a flush of success as the X-rays produce images. But there are other X-rays or other image-producing devices, and they produce different images. In the case of semiotics and literary criticism, we are inclined to accept this, even to treat it as a kind of historical fate, and to drop notions such as explanation, determinacy, causality, teleology and the like entirely. Along with the idea of determinate interpretation, of course, goes the 'presuppositions' model, for unless there is something determinate – such as a meaning – there is no hidden collective thing, such as a set of shared presuppositions, that can be inferred from its existence.
4 In, for example, David Lockwood, *Solidarity and Schism: 'The Problem of Disorder in Durkheimian and Marxist Sociology'* (Clarendon Press, Oxford, 1992).
5 Alasdair MacIntyre, *Whose Justice? Which Rationality?* (University of Notre Dame Press, Notre Dame, IN, 1988).

6 Richard Rorty, 'Deconstruction and circumvention', *Critical Inquiry*, 11 (1984), p. 3.
7 Some texts, of which Wittgenstein's scraps may be given as an example, themselves proceed largely in terms of what might be described as a rhetoric in which the main effect of the text is in making sense of the bits of reasoning and forming the habits that enable one to do so more easily. These texts avoid the explicit drawing of 'conclusions' or the advancing of 'theses', and in this way force the reader to acquire new habits or give up. Other texts do this to a different, but usually smaller, extent. Forming a reader or listener in this way is hard work on both sides.
8 The idea that interpreters change their 'theories' in order to understand sayings of the persons they are interpreting is advanced by Donald Davidson, with radical results similar to my conclusions in this book. Cf. 'A Nice Derangement of Epitaphs', in E. LePore ed., *Truth and Interpretation: Perspectives on the Philosophy of Donald Davidson*, (Basil Blackwell, Oxford, 1986), p. 442. Davidson suggests that, 'What people need if they are to understand one another through speech, is the ability to converge on passing theories [by which he means the revised tacit premisses that enable them to understand what they did not at first understand] from utterance to utterance. Their starting points, however far back we want to take them, will usually be very different – as different as the ways in which they acquired their linguistic skills. So also, then, will the strategies and stratagems that bring about convergence differ' (p. 445). He concludes that 'we must give up the idea of a clearly defined structure which language-users acquire and then apply to cases', i.e., the idea of a language as traditionally conceived, because there is 'no such thing to be learned, mastered, or born with' (p. 446). I agree with this conclusion. My grounds for doing so differ, in that I have focused on the problem of getting a theory of transmission. It is instructive that responses to Davidson, such as Ian Hacking's 'The parody of conversation' (in the same volume), appeal to the same locational devices I have tried here to show are highly problematic, such as 'community' (p. 458). Michael Dummett argues that there are ways to avoid the implications of the claim that 'language consists of an individual's "habits of speech when addressing a particular hearer" at a particular time' (p. 469), such as a distinction between a 'short-range' and 'long-range' sense of language such that the older project can be preserved as it applied to the long-range sense, meaning the more stable body of usage from which idiolects deviate (usually temporarily). The problem of transmission, I would argue, is fatal to this distinction. There is no transmittable thing of this sort, no place to put it, and no causal processes that put it there. All that 'long-range' can mean is useful for understanding more people, over longer time periods.
9 Cf. Stephen Turner, 'Tacit knowledge and the problem of computer modelling cognitive processes in science', in S. Fuller, Marc de Mey, Terry Shinn and Steve Woolgar, eds, *The Cognitive Turn: Sociological and*

Psychological Perspectives on Science (Reidel, Dordrecht, 1989). I hope the argument here is sufficient to distinguish my views from those of writers like Harry Collins, who develop what is in the end an essentialist account of human thought in support of the claim that it cannot be emulated by computers.

Index

abridgements 93, 95
addition 70, 110
agreement 59-77 *passim*, 120
  'brute fact' of 72
  rule creation through 133
Alexander, J. 130
American gait 20-4
Anglo-Saxon origins 5, 81
Annales School 35, 38
anthropologists 2, 4, 27
apprenticeship 64-5
artificial intelligence 1, 11-13, 97, 101, 117, 123, 133
'as if' formulations 32, 36, 72
associationist theory of learning 18
assumptions 29-35, 102
  attributions of 31, 33
  basic 85
  as hypotheses 34
  as psychological reality 32
  see also presuppositions
atheism 122

Austin, J. 14-16, 18-20, 24, 25, 94, 126
Australian Aborigines 91, 132-3
Azande 90, 118-19, 133

background, inherited 1-2, 11, 68-9, 73, 133
Barnes, B. 134
Beck, A. 131
behaviourism 6, 15
belief 2, 4, 7, 28-30, 33-4, 54, 84, 87, 122
  religious 118-19, 121-2
Bell, D. 124
Bellah, R. 77
Bentham, J. 25
Berkeley, G. 6, 7, 19, 41, 66, 125
biological causes and descriptions 16, 22-3, 26
  matched to behaviour 23, 110
body 58-9, 98
  techniques of 20-3, 126

Botwinich, A. 130
Bourdieu, P. 1, 27, 37, 47–8, 50, 62, 77, 93, 115, 124
bourgeoisie 4
Burckhardt, J. 5, 12, 34–41, 127

Calvin, J. 61, 114
Calvin and Calvinism 61, 114
Camic, C. 126
capacities 41–2, 46, 49, 126
 diminished 91
 see also language and linguistic, competencies and capacities
 innate 46
carpentry 96–7
causal inference 7, 9, 12, 19, 30
causal structure of practices 6, 8, 11–13, 15, 22, 42, 45, 49, 53
 of habits 105
Cavell, S. 121
change, explanation of 83–6, 89, 129
 see also closure
charisma 131
Chomsky, N. 19
Christ 68–9, 130
Christianity and Christian life 68–9, 73, 92, 107, 133
Cicero 6, 21
Cicourel, A. 39
circadian rhythms 16
classes, social 14, 20, 85, 95, 112, 128
closure 86, 89–91, 133
code model 46, 85–6, 90, 92
cognitive therapy 131
collective consciousness 25, 51–5, 57, 78, 115
collective effervescence 64
collective objects, hidden 123, 134
 practices as 100, 102, 104–5, 110, 114–16; *see also* practices, as objects
 traditions as 99–100
Collins, H. 127, 130, 136
communication 68–9, 120
Communism 80–1
community 1, 36, 54, 70–1, 74–5, 78–9, 99, 117, 135
 interpretive 54, 87–8
comprehension *see* understanding
constitution 102
 American 93
 British 14, 20, 25, 95
constitutionalism 5
construction, social 9, 12, 38, 83, 104
conventions 3–4, 11, 56–8, 60, 62, 108, 110
 interpretive 62
 possession of 60, 62
conversational analysis 12, 39–40, 43
convict code 54, 129
cosmology 91–2
Critical Theory and Critical Theorists 4
culture 3, 6, 20–7 *passim*, 35, 37, 46, 60, 68–9, 77–9, 82, 87, 103–4, 112, 121, 132
 facticity of 39
 instrumental value of concept of 27, 78–9
 political 6, 20, 111, 113
 scientific 4, 10
 tacit part of 113
 as unified whole 79
customs 3, 5–7, 9, 12, 24, 36, 49, 68, 93, 103, 125, 129
 as second nature 6, 21

Dasein 1
Davidson, D. 135
deMey, M. 135
democracy 5–6, 94, 117
demonstration effects 92
Deng Xiaoping 80–1
Derrida, J. 63
deviance and deviation 26, 70–1, 75
Dewey, J. 126
dialectics 89
discipline 58, 61–2, 76–7, 126
dispositions 3, 30, 43, 47, 50, 62
diversity of morals, customs and practices 1, 7, 9–10, 12, 49, 102
Dreyfus, H. 1, 124
Dummett, M. 135
Durkheim, E. 5, 20, 24–5, 27, 28, 35, 38, 51–5, 64, 65, 71, 73, 77, 104, 108, 114–16, 128, 129, 134

economics 28, 32–3
economists 114
education 105
egalitarianism 95–6
Eliade, M. 91–2, 107, 132
Eliot, T. S. 77, 93, 94, 133
Elster, J. 3, 125
embeddedness 11, 40, 43, 54, 87, 123, 128
emigration 80, 131
emotional responses 107, 114
emulation 82, 92, 97–9, 105–6, 109–11, 117, 123, 126
  as substitute for transmission 98
epistemes 84
epistemology, naturalization of 10

error 121–2
essences and essentialism 45, 96, 136
ethics 102
  group 129
  see also morals and morality
ethnicity 80
ethnomethodology 12, 38–43, 51, 127–8, 129
Europe, Eastern 80
Evans-Pritchard, E. E. 90, 118, 132, 133
evolution, social 4–5
evolutionism 83
expectations 21, 24, 35–7, 81, 99, 123
explanation 11, 24
  end-point to 45
  functionalist 28, 83, 114
  see also causal structure of practices; inference to the best explanation; teleology
external world 86

fact-value distinction 4
feedback 59, 74–5, 90, 109
feminism 1, 95, 134
fictiveness 45
Fish, S. 53–5, 86, 87, 88–91, 92, 94, 96, 103, 129-30 132, 133
Fischer, D. 80, 131
'forms of life' *see Lebensformen*
Foucault, M. 35, 55, 62, 77, 84, 108, 126, 129
foundations 7, 9
framework 2, 79, 121
Freeman, A. 131
Freud, S. 130
Freudians 133
Fuller, S. 135
Fuller, T. 133

Index

functionalism *see* explanation, functionalist; holism; teleology

Gadamer, H.-G.   2, 125, 131
Gardiner, P.   34, 127
Gardner, A.   133
Garfinkel, H.   127–8
Geertz, C.   90, 132
gender and gendering   1
Germanic tribes *see* Anglo-Saxon origins
Germans and Germany   5, 20, 133
Gillen, F.   132
Goodman, N.   86
Gopnik, M.   126
grammar   19, 69, 99, 125
  gene for   103, 126
'grasping'   50, 69–72, 93
Greek oracles   90
Groves, L.   106
Gumperz, J.   127

habit and habituation   7–8, 12–19, 21–2, 26, 42, 57–9, 61, 76–123 *passim*, 126
  acquisition of   105–6, 109, 122
  causal features of   16–19, 21–2, 26, 50, 59, 105
  force of   52, 59
  of mind   16–18, 56, 62, 107
  of moderation   14–16, 20, 24
habitus   1, 47, 50, 78, 93, 116
Hacking, I.   135
Hegel, G. W. F.   5
hegemony *see* power, hegemonic
Heidegger, M.   1, 124
Hilbert, R.   128
historicity   2, 4, 36, 38, 45
Hobbes, T.   6, 26, 114, 130

Hobsbawm, E.   131
Hoch, P.   131
holism
  causal   107
  cultural   25
horizons   103, 123, 131
Hume, D.   6–8, 9, 12, 19, 30, 49, 68, 93, 103, 125, 129
Husserl, E.   124
Hymes, D.   127

ideology   2–3, 24, 29, 49, 56, 61, 80, 107
  of a class   85
  habitualization of   83, 131
Ihering, R.   5, 25, 101
imitation   21, 44–5, 48, 61, 64, 66
implantation   31, 44, 51
inaccessibility of practices and traditions   80–5, 90, 96, 107
  as cause of persistence   87
incommensurability   85, 93
individualism   26, 81
inference to the best explanation   13, 18, 115
information   85–6, 97, 126
initiation   82, 96
inscription metaphor   3, 17–18, 37, 120
institutions, total   106
insufficiency argument   10, 78, 101–2
intention and intentionality   1–2, 70, 72, 111, 129
  collective   51, 54–5, 59, 129
  tacit   60
  see also purposes
interpretation, theory of   13, 102
interpretive correctness   9, 45, 62, 65
introjection   6, 48, 50, 115, 130

intuitionism, moral 17
Iser, W. 64, 74, 129, 130

Jesuit education 106
judgement 8, 125, 132
Jugendweihe 81

Kant, I. 5, 8, 29, 30–1, 125–6, 127, 132
Kennedy, J. F. 46
knowing how and knowing what 2
knowledge engineering 98
Kripke, S. 68–77, 110, 130, 131, 133
Kuhn, T. 2, 3, 83–4, 86, 92
Kwakiutl 33

language 2, 59–60, 82, 86
  private 68–9
language and linguistic 2, 6, 13, 42, 59, 95, 103, 121, 125, 135
  competencies and capacities 3, 19, 40, 46, 65
  first and second 42, 65, 82, 93
law and lawyers 2–3, 5, 10–11, 25–6, 38, 101–2, 125, 130, 133
Lebensformen 1, 68–71 *passim*, 93–4, 130, 131, 133
LeBon, G. 64, 130
Lecky, W. 17
LePore, E. 135
Le Suicide (Durkheim) 35
Lévi-Strauss, C. 67, 90–1, 133
Lewis, D. 2–3, 125
literary criticism 1, 128
literary theory 104, 129–30
location 40, 49–77 *passim*, 103, 120, 135
  in collective mind 56

collective object solutions 50, 56–7
  dualistic solutions 50–5, 60–1
  private solutions 57
Lockwood, D. 134
Lynch, M. 127

Macfarlane, A. 81, 131
Machiavelli, N. 130
MacIntyre 2, 82, 93, 117, 125, 131, 134
Mannheim 134
Marshall, T. 116
Martian biologist 21–2
Marx, K. 27, 116, 134
Marxism 4–5, 133, 134
  literary 134
mathematics 108–11
  elementary 68–72
  reality of objects of 109
  truths of 109
Mauss, M. 20, 21–6, 33, 47, 50, 73, 123, 126
Maussian problem 19–24, 33, 36, 38, 123
Mead, G. 116
mental objects 15
  shared 5, 50
mentalités 30, 35–6, 47, 115
Merleau-Ponty, M. 134
milieu 54
mind
  objective 69
  social 25
Montesquieu, C. 114
morals and morality 4–6, 17, 19, 24, 26, 51, 61, 64, 102
  see also customs; diversity of morals; *mores*; practices
mores 4, 25–8, 78, 80–3, 93, 96, 98–9, 116, 127

causal traits of 25
mutuality 50, 52, 59, 74–5, 78, 105
social 25

nature
human 6, 10, 21–2, 103, 125
second 103
nature vs. culture 103–5, 110
neo-Kantianism 4–5, 83
Nietzsche, F. 44, 64, 127, 128
Nisbet, R. 132
norms 3–4, 25, 28, 47, 64–5, 78–9, 102, 116
Nyíri, J. 125

Oakeshott, M. 2, 77, 93, 95, 124–5, 130, 133
observances 94, 97, 99, 104–7, 117
as cause of habits 99–100, 104, 107–8
ensembles of 106, 112
religious 118
order and orderliness 35–43 *passim*, 127–8
organic vocabulary 15, 19, 25, 114–15
Ortner, S. 124

paradigm 2, 60, 78–9, 82–5, 93, 123
shifts 83–4
Pareto, V. 116
Parliament 14, 94
Parsons, T. 4, 50, 77, 114, 115
Pascal, B. 6
Peckham, M. 128
performance, sameness of 42, 58–9, 66, 76, 97–8, 105
persistence 13, 18, 24, 38, 45, 57, 59, 78–9, 81–2, 87, 98–9, 105, 113
anomalous 79, 81
persuasion 8, 88, 111
phenomenology 107, 109
philosophy 1–3, 7–10, 49, 57, 68, 82, 100–1, 104
physics 106
Pickering, A. 127
Plato 63, 67, 130
Polanyi, M. 2, 3, 64, 77, 125, 133
political theory and theorists 5, 29, 121
politics 3, 117
Roman 10
Pollner, M. 39
Porter, R. 129
Poster, M. 5, 62, 77, 129
postmodernism 2, 4
power 13, 108–9, 111–13, 125, 128, 134
hegemonic 57, 108–9, 111, 113
practice 8, 95, 125
practice, learning by 6, 19, 41–2, 65
practice theory 2
practices *passim*
acquisition of *see* transmission
bi-level structure of 15, 49–50
identification and discovery of 12, 20–4, 37, 46
instrumental concept of 37, 98
intersubstitutability with principles 6–7, 9, 12, 45, 122–3
as objects 13, 15, 19–20, 24, 59–69, 64, 100; *see also* collective objects, hidden
philosophical uses of 1–3, 7–8, 44

predictive use of 36–7
sharing of 1–2, 11–13, 30, 58–60, 64, 77, 104
vs. practice 8
see also causal structure of practices
'practice-reproduction' model 48
pragmatism and pragmatists 16
preferences, revealed 28, 114
presuppositions 2–4, 12, 29–30, 47, 62, 90, 96, 103, 120–3, 127, 134
  fundamental 118
  interdependence of skill and 3
  as psychological fact 29–35, 37, 121, 127
  shared 12, 31, 34
principles 7, 8, 12
  generative 39
  grounding 10
  ultimate 7
Protestant Ethic and the Spirit of Capitalism, The (Weber) 61
psychologists 48
psychotherapy 106
purposes 28, 62, 89–90, 129
  collective 55, 88–90, 93, 129
  common social 51–2
  of community 87, 132

quaddition 70, 110
Quine, W. V. O. 2, 10, 19, 58, 125

race 5
Ranger, T. 131
rational choice theorists 114
rationality 13
rationalization 131–2
reason, universal 10, 49

reception 62, 64, 88, 129–30
  capacity for 67
reflexivity 32, 38
Reichenbach, H. 51–2, 128
relativism 2, 5, 13
  cultural 4
  historical 2
  practice 118–23
relics 34–6, 41
religious experience 106
representation, practices of 1, 2, 38–9, 95, 126
representations 51, 54
  collective 58, 65, 104
reproduction 13–14, 47–8, 45, 62, 77, 111, 115, 128
  of distinctions 1
  psychological account of 47
rhetoric and rhetorical practices 1, 45, 135
risk 26
ritual 2, 91, 117–18
Rorty, R. 2, 86, 120–1, 125, 135
routines 3, 26, 43, 111
rules 6, 15, 19, 41, 50–1, 56–8, 65, 67–77, 79, 83, 87, 93, 97, 110, 117, 125–6 132

'rules model of culture' 68–9, 73, 83, 88
Ryle, G. 2, 125

Sacks, H. 39–42, 127
Said, E. 1
'same transmission, same acquisition' model 65-6
sameness 12–13, 19, 26, 40, 56, 58, 61, 77 *passim*, 79–80, 84, 93, 96–8, 103–5
  see also performance, sameness of

Schütz, A. 134
science 1, 3–4, 10, 16, 38, 65, 77, 80, 83, 92, 131
  conceptual change in 13
  history of 121
  as source of imagery 53–4, 73
science studies 1, 12
Seiler, L. 128
self-interest 4
sentiment, habitualization of 18, 20
Septuagint 67
sewing 8
Shils, E. 64
Shinn, T. 135
signifiers 35, 134
Simmel, G. 64
Sitten 5, 102–3, 125
skills 3, 10–11, 58–9, 65, 97, 132, 135
  see also presuppositions, interdependence of skills and
Smith, B. 125
Smith, P. 130
social, the 2, 9, 12
social change 45, 132
social determination 123
social fact 5, 24, 38, 50
social theory 1, 5–6, 11–12, 15, 57, 100, 103–4, 113–18, 128, 131, 134
socialization 6, 64, 78
society 24–5, 54, 103, 114, 123, 128
  conceived anthropomorphically 54–5
sociology and sociologists 4–5, 64, 83, 132
  of knowledge 4, 29
Socrates 67
Socratic dialogue 32

sorcery 90–1, 132
Sorokin, P. 132
Spencer, B. 132
Spencer, H. 4
Spranger, E. 1, 68–9, 73, 107, 130, 133
Stammler, R. 127
stateways and folkways 80–1, 105
suicide rates 115
Sumner, G. 6, 25–7, 82–3, 93, 99, 105, 127
superego 6
systems 86, 89
  cultural 121
Szilard, L. 106

tacit knowledge 2–3, 8, 11, 46–7, 56, 65, 97, 102–3, 117
Tacitus 81
Taine, H. 5
Tarde, G. 44
teaching, acquisition through 45, 58
techniques 20–3, 40, 62
  power/knowledge 55, 108
teleology 25, 116
tests 71, 75, 130
texts 57, 61–4, 102, 129
  habit-inducing 121, 135
textualism 57
theism 121–2
theology 3, 42
'theory' analogy 119
theory of the world 2, 99, 121
Tönnies, F. 5, 25, 51–5, 59, 71, 73, 77, 114, 125, 129
Tracy, D. 56
tradition 2–3, 15, 24, 78–85 *passim*, 93, 98, 100, 103, 107, 117, 133

British vs. German and
  American 117
continuity of 96
essences 96
invented 81
lack of 96–7, 133
political 77, 93–4, 102, 117
possession of 95
as tacit object 97
transcendental arguments 34
translation 46, 82, 85, 92, 96
transmission 12–13, 43–77,
  79–80, 90, 92, 98, 103, 113,
  136
  as marination 117; *see also*
    agreement; code model;
    'grasping'; implantation;
    introjection
  mechanisms of 50–2
  perfect 66, 76
  privileged form 63–4
  reproductive 48
  sameness preserving 103
  through participation 47
treaty 60–2
truth 1–2, 9–10, 45, 107, 118
  ultimate 119
Turner, S. 135

Überbau 85
underdetermination 30–1, 43,
  102, 110
understanding 26, 68, 75, 104,
  109, 122, 130

Unger, R. 3, 125, 134
utilitarianism 17, 25, 129

values 9, 27–8, 36, 83, 131
  objective 130
Veblen, T. 107
verbalization 32–3
Victorian sexuality 84–5
Vietnam War Memorial 107

Wagner, R. 94
Watson, G. 128
Weber, M. 5, 9, 26, 61–2, 83–4,
  114, 116, 127, 128, 131–2
Wellington, Duke of 106
Weltanschauung 5, 12, 29–30,
  34–43 *passim*, 78, 82, 84, 103,
  114
Wieder, D. 55, 89, 127–8, 129
Wilson, W. 81
Winch, P. 130, 133
Wittgenstein, L. 1, 2, 50, 56,
  68–73, 75, 93, 94, 110, 124,
  127, 128–9, 130, 131, 133, 135
Wolfe, T. 81
Woolgar, S. 127, 135–6
world picture 1–2, 11
world view *see Weltanschauung*
Woschnak, W. 125

Xenophon 67

Yearley, S. 127

Lightning Source UK Ltd.
Milton Keynes UK
UKOW01f1603110416

272013UK00001B/22/P